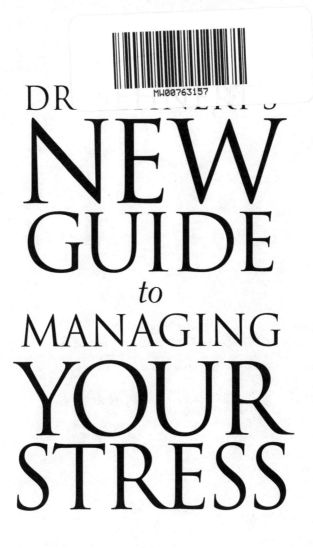

DR SEHNERT'S
NEW
GUIDE
to
MANAGING
YOUR
STRESS

Keith W. Sehnert, M.D.

Augsburg

MINNEAPOLIS

Cover design: Michael Mihelich
Book design: Elizabeth Boyce

ISBN 0-8066-3595-9

Manufactured in the U.S.A.   AF 9-3595

04   03   02   01   00   99   98   1   2   3   4   5   6   7   8

CONTENTS

PREFACE

My book *Stress/Unstress* was published in 1981, and since then more than three hundred thousand readers have learned from it how to handle the stresses of everyday life. Then recently my niece asked me, "When are you going to write *Stress/Unstress II?*" Soon thereafter I called Ron Klug, at that time director of publishing for Augsburg Books, and set up an appointment to discuss a new book. He was interested, and I sent him my outline for the proposed book. When he discussed the outline with his staff, one of them said, "You mean they had stress in 1981?" When the laughter died down, all agreed the book idea was a go.

No doubt stress is more common now. Divorce rates remain high; bankruptcy is more common; job changes from downsizing and business mergers are way up. Our bodies absorb more air and water pollution from vehicles and industries, more noise from loud music, traffic, and airplanes, and fewer nutrients in our highly processed and preserved foods. In more families both parents work outside the home, and more adults remain single. We are working longer days, with more commuting time, more pressure to increase production, and less leisure time for family and friends. It's a life of *hurry, hurry, hurry.*

In addition to these changes there is the emotional turmoil from crime and violence. It's just plain hazardous to turn on your TV set! All you hear is trouble, trouble, and more trouble, so that one of my doctor friends advises "TV fasting"—no TV for one week!

6   With all those scary things out there, it's easy to become upset about the external and internal stressors, but, as I've told thousands of the readers of my fifteen books about medical self-care and the many patients I've treated in the past few years, "All of us are getting smarter." There are obstacles to overcome, but you can use the brain that the Lord gave you. Work with your family, friends, fellow workers, clergy, and counselors. Remember another old adage, "All of us are smarter than any one of us!" As a student, family doctor, husband, father, and Christian layperson, I have learned about the power of prayer and the strength of friends and family. I have been a mentor, but I have also been mentored by many others — including my patients.

First and foremost among my mentors is my dear wife, Colleen. Throughout the writing of this book — and the others I've written — she has served as M.C., or Master Clarifier, responding with key questions such as "What do you mean here?" or comments such as "I don't think this is clear." So, a special thanks to you, Coke.

I also want to give a special thanks to Ron Klug for carefully critiquing the manuscript and making many useful suggestions. These made the book better in many ways. Thanks, Ron.

I also want to thank dear friends, William G. Crook, M.D., and Joan Mathews Larson, Ph.D., for their reviews of the manuscript.

Now, it is my fervent prayer that you are ready to learn what stress experts have discovered in recent years. Practice the useful tips suggested here, not just by "Dr. Keith," but by other experts from around the world. You can't avoid all the stressors of life, but with God's help you can learn to manage your stress and live a more healthy, happy, and productive life.

Keith W. Selment, MD

PART ONE:
UNDERSTANDING
STRESS

CASUALTIES OF STRESS: WILL YOU BE ONE?

1

When the experts talk about the casualties of stress, one thing that always puzzles them is that our reactions to it can vary so widely, depending on the stress. What is it about stress that makes people get a little sick, with, say, a headache or acid stomach, while at other times they might get more sick, with a bad case of the flu or enough indigestion to turn into a stomach ulcer, or even very sick, requiring a trip to the emergency room or worse. You might get a little sick from stress when someone quits at your office, so you have to work until 8:00 P.M. all week. By the weekend you've come down with a serious cold. A more serious stressor might result in a more serious illness.

For an example of this I don't have to search my patient files, I just look at my own. When I was a young family doctor in York, Nebraska, I was on emergency call one Saturday. I knew I could be called to the York County Fairgrounds because the State Flying Farmers Convention was being held that day. I was reading the sports page of the *Omaha World-Herald*. The feature story was about a western Nebraska football star who had just received a scholarship to play with the Cornhuskers. The photo showed a handsome, smiling, red-haired quarterback. Just then, the call came. A plane had crashed and burned at the fairgrounds.

I ran to my car and hurried to the airport near the fairgrounds where the firemen had already put out the blaze. The sheriff and I cautiously approached the wreckage. The pilot, an older man, was dead and burned beyond recognition. The

10   passenger, who I learned was the pilot's nephew, was not as badly burned, but he was dead by the time we reached him. He had bright red hair and a face I quickly recognized. He was the football player whose picture I had seen in the paper.

After the shock wore off and the bodies were removed from the wreckage and put into the waiting ambulance, it was my duty to call the families of the victims. No one was home at the pilot's residence, so I called the young man's home. His mother answered the phone. I tried to make my voice as sympathetic as I could, but I had to say, "Your son has been killed in a plane crash." I comforted her as best I could, but I'll never forget her voice or the sobs that followed. "O Lord, how could that happen? Why? Why?"

Even before I hung up, my stomach started reacting. There was a terrible acid taste in my mouth. By the time I finished the police reports, there was a gnawing pain in my belly. By midnight I had so much pain I couldn't sleep. I had developed a stomach ulcer. The doctor was now a patient! Fortunately, the ulcer healed over the next several weeks, but I had learned firsthand what it meant to get sick from stress.

A friend shared a story about stress causing even more serious harm. Her neighbor had experienced a double tragedy. First, her mother died. Then, twelve days later, her father died. The shock of his wife's death had been so severe that her father, a farmer who had no known health problems, died on the way to the post office of an apparent heart attack. So their entire family was back in the same rural church for a second funeral. Everyone in their little farm town was shocked by the news.

When the events were pieced together, what had happened became more clear. For nearly six months the farmer (we'll call him Mr. Jones) had cared for his severely ill wife. In addition, he did all the regular farm chores. His eating habits were dreadful, according to a neighbor. He slept poorly, because he had to help his wife use the bathroom several times every night. Then, after thirty-five years of marriage, his wife died. The strain and

stress was too much for him. This is a classic example of deadly
serious stress.

These stories—the bad cold, my ulcer pain, and the sudden death of the farmer—help us to begin to understand the "casualties of stress." Naturally, we wonder how we can prevent problems related to stress. But before you read on, ask yourself if your body is already talking to you. Has it been a really bad year? A rotten month? Has stress put you at risk for health problems from overload? You can begin to find out by taking the "Quick Quiz" below. Finish the quiz and count your yes answers. If your score is three or more, you will have to be extra vigilant.

Quick Quiz: Are You at Risk?

Answer the following questions with respect to the past twelve months.

1. Has stress been extremely bad? (Have you experienced one or more of the following: the death of a spouse, parent, or child; divorce or marital separation; being fired from a job; business readjustment, promotion, or demotion; change in living conditions?)

2. Do you abuse caffeine, nicotine, or alcohol? (Do you drink more than five cups of coffee or five cans of cola per day? Do you smoke more than five cigarettes, cigars, or pipes per day? Do you drink more than two glasses of wine, two bottles or cans of beer, or two ounces of hard liquor per day?)

3. Has the air quality been worse than last year at work or home? (Are you around more smokers, car fumes, diesel odors, moldy odors, solvents, or chemicals?)

4. Has something in your food or water made you ill? (Do you have food sensitivities such as allergies to milk or dairy products, wheat, peanuts, chocolate, or strawberries? Are you sensitive to amino acid tyrosine in aged cheese? Are there other additives in your food, such as sulfites, nitrates,

or MSG? Have you noticed a bad metallic taste to your drinking water? Is your tap water heavily chlorinated?)

5. Are you more sedentary, becoming more of a "couch potato"? Do you exercise less than three times weekly for twenty minutes?

6. Have you used broad-spectrum antibiotics—such as tetracycline, Keflex®, ampicillin, amoxicillin, Ceclor®, Bactrim®, or Septra®—either for two weeks in a row or four different times? After taking an antibiotic, have you had recurrent sinus problems, vaginitis, vaginal discharge, diarrhea, thrush in mouth, or allergic reaction?

7. Are you taking corticosteroids—such as prednisone, Decadron®, or other cortisone-type drugs—for asthma, bowel condition, arthritis, or chronic allergies?

8. Are you taking oral contraceptives (birth control pills) or progesterone?

9. Do you have athlete's foot, ringworm, jock itch, or chronic fungus infections of skin, nails, toes, or hands?

10. Do you experience excessive fatigue, feel drained of energy, "spacey," or forgetful, or have more moodiness or depression than usual?

TOTAL _____

Next, I'd like to give you the case history of John Doe, who lives in our neighborhood. As I write this at 7:30 A.M., I can see him walking to the bus stop.

John has a good job. He is happily married. Everyone likes him, but there are some problems that concern his wife and family doctor. John lost the "Battle of the Bulge" when he was forty, and he is now forty-five pounds overweight. He drinks eight cups of coffee each day and can't get through the evening without at least two cans of beer. After puffing on Marlboros for over fifteen years, he quit smoking last year, but now he smokes a few cigarettes on his way to and from work. He covers up smoker's breath with mint candy, so his wife won't suspect. John is president of the local Couch Potatoes Club and stirs from the davenport only when the Vikings get ahead of the Green Bay Packers or the Chicago Bears. He takes blood-pressure pills regularly, but he forgets his thyroid medication most of the time, and he frequently needs a sleeping pill prescribed by his doctor.

Like Mr. Jones, John is very vulnerable to a major stress, such as a job loss or family problems. He doesn't have *reserve power*, the ability to fend off a common cold virus or recover from a normally minor life event. Hans Selye, the father of modern-day stress research, called John's condition "distressed syndrome."[1] Dr. Jeffrey Bland, author of *The 20-Day Rejuvenation Diet Program*, calls it the "walking wounded syndrome."[2]

So when this neighbor of mine crosses the street for another day of work, what risks does he face? I have identified them with "trouble arrows" on the diagram below. One or several risks can further decrease John's reserve power. They can alter the normal immune responses and natural healing ability of his body.

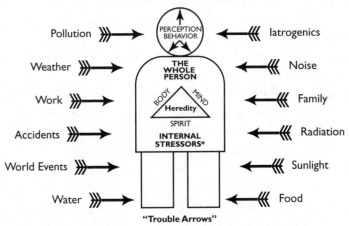

EXTERNAL STRESSORS

Pollution	Iatrogenics
Weather	Noise
Work	Family
Accidents	Radiation
World Events	Sunlight
Water	Food

PERCEPTION BEHAVIOR

THE WHOLE PERSON

BODY / MIND / Heredity / SPIRIT

INTERNAL STRESSORS*

"Trouble Arrows"

* Nutritional stress, food intolerances, bacteria/viral/fungal (yeast) infections, hormonal dysfunction (thyroid, adrenals, pituitary, etc.), caffeine/nicotine/alcohol/medications

14   Is poor John doomed? Is there a time bomb waiting to explode? Should he just give up any efforts to correct his negative lifestyles?

The answer, of course, is no. That's what this book is all about. Since 1981, when *Stress/Unstress* was published, a mountain of exciting new research has given us new insights into the way stress works. We've learned a lot about improving your reserve power. There's new information about how to handle—or, better yet, avoid—many of the trouble arrows, or health risks of stress.

Remember, if you had three or more yes answers on the Quick Quiz, your reserve power may be diminished, and you may be at increased risk for stress-related problems. A high score doesn't mean you are ill or that some minor stress or life event will cause you to collapse. On the other hand, what you normally cope with could make you more irritable and uptight. This puts you at risk and impairs your body's healing ability.

For instance, when Mr. Jones was not eating regularly and later stopped eating altogether, essential vitamins and minerals were not available for everyday repair work in his body. During the several months that he cared for his wife, his sleep was poor. Later on his daughter reported that his diesel pickup had not been working well. He would leave it running in the barn while doing work there, subjecting himself to air pollution. So in addition to the emotional stress associated with his wife's death, there were other trouble arrows pointing at him. His reserve power was being compromised. His "at risk" score was high.

What about that neighbor of mine on the street corner waiting for the bus? John hasn't crashed yet, but there are some new warning signs. A man who worked at the same Fortune 500 company as John told me that he had seen John the previous week and that he hadn't looked good. He had asked John if he had been ill or to the doctor, and John said, "Oh, I'm O.K. My wife and doctor are on my tail, but I'll be fine. I'm going to start walking more—if I have time." The lines "I'm O.K." and "If I have time" are part of the denial syndrome that is very popular among forty-something males. It is revealed by statements such as, "I can eat what I want" or "A little beer and a few cigarettes never hurt anybody."

This denial syndrome can begin early on, especially among males. Young boys are often told "big boys don't cry" or "keep a stiff upper lip." In the process of growing up they suffer in silence. A pattern of ignoring "body talk" (physical symptoms) indicating something is affecting them adversely is established. Habits, both good and bad, are difficult to break. John is not alone!

As I reflect on the many patients I've seen in my years as a family doctor, I'm reminded of a patient I saw when I ran Georgetown's Reston-Herndon Medical Center in Virginia, a few miles from Washington, D.C. The patient was a retired coal miner from West Virginia. He described a unique safety device that miners had used many years ago. Before today's mining safety gauges were developed, the old-timers would take a caged canary down into the mine shaft with them at the start of the day. If the shaft contained a poisonous gas such as methane, the canary would be affected by it long before the men were. When it fell off its perch onto the floor of the cage, that signaled trouble, and the miners would drop their picks and run out to fresh air.

Perhaps one of these days scientists will develop an electronic device that will serve as a kind of stress canary. Meanwhile, you'll have to rely on your own intelligence. I'll provide you with enough tips and information in the chapters that follow to keep your canary from falling onto the floor!

2 | THE STRESS OF "FREE LUNCHES"

Milton Friedman, Nobel Prize laureate in economics and former professor at Stanford University and the University of Chicago, first made the comment, "There's no such thing as a free lunch!"[1] I have observed this many times in my medical career. Often we eventually have to pay for things that were initially thought to be cost-free innovations. My cousin, Erling Podoll of Frederick, South Dakota, a long-time employee with the U.S.D.A. Soil Conservation Service, says it another way: "Private gain, public pay."[2]

Here are some examples of the "free lunches" that we pay for, causing stress now, in A.D. 2000, and beyond for ourselves and our communities.

Chemicals and Pesticides in Agriculture

The classic example of expensive "progress" is the weed killer, DDT. Although now banned in the United States, it is still widely used in Central and South America and throughout the Third World. When it was first introduced to American farmers in the 1950s, it was hailed as a win-win breakthrough: fewer weeds, more crops, less work. It was a thought to be a free lunch, but was it? In *Silent Spring*, published in 1962, Rachel Carson noted that DDT kills not only weeds but also the birds who eat them. Irvine T. Dietrich, a soil conservationist affiliated with North Dakota State University, said at the time, "If the chemists persist in their poisonous methods, they must invent more and stronger poisons to deal with the resistance nature sets up against them. In this way a vicious cycle is created!"

After Carson's warning, doctors began to attribute to DDT and its poisonous descendants an increased incidence of birth defects among newborns. For example, in 1952, before DDT was widely used, there were 20,000 such cases. By 1958 there were 60,000. In 1964, there were 126,000 and by 1968 more than 500,000, according to Peter Tompkins and Christopher Bird in their book *The Secret Life of Plants*.[3] If a child born in the 1950s or 1960s was handicapped because of DDT, families, communities, and states paid a big price.

Recent studies found DDT particles as far away as the ice caps of the South Pole. The DDT had floated in the air across the equator and landed in Antarctica. Theresa Podoll of the Northern Plains Sustainable Agricultural Society, an organic farming cooperative in North Dakota, said they also found Aldrin and Dieldrin, common pesticides.[4]

Faulty Home Construction

Since 1970 more energy-efficient homes and schools have been built, but these, too, have proven to have unforeseen costs. If your children and teenagers are spending the same twenty-five to twenty-six hours a week in "sick" schools and ninety or so hours in the homes that reek of mold and other chemicals, then you had better blow the whistle—and blow it loud!

In the fall of 1997 the *Star Tribune* in Minneapolis carried a series of articles on this problem.[5] The first dealt with what has happened in thousands of so-called energy-efficient homes in the Twin Cities and across the nation. Since 1970, attempts have been made to tighten the shells of homes in order to cut heating and cooling costs. This has made them more susceptible to moisture problems and rot. The composite wood products most often used (wafer board, chip board, and "O.S.B.") deteriorate rapidly on exposure to moisture. The article states,

18   "These problems reflect a state of building codes that lag behind scientific knowledge concerning how to build durable healthy homes." Hans Hagen, a spokesman for the Minnesota Builders Association, observed, "For an awful lot of years we built houses and they worked just fine, and they stood for 100 or 150 years. And then, all of a sudden our modern society said . . . we need to conserve energy . . . and it had an impact on the structured durability of the houses . . . and we're dealing with that."

Are these findings only for homes in Minnesota or do homeowners from Maine to Washington also have to worry? Observers from elsewhere in the United States say the problem is common. One expert from Boston said, "The builders ignored the need for getting fresh air into homes to control moisture and protect occupant health." When families experience moisture problems—wet windows, cracked walls, damp basements, bad smells, and popped nails—the stress isn't only on their nerves, but also on their pocketbooks.

The last article in this series focused on the effects of moisture on the health of the children who live in these homes. The reporters found a high incidence of asthma, respiratory ailments, earaches, and skin rashes caused by mold. Molds release substances called mycotoxins, which when inhaled can cause damage to vital organs and the body's immune system.

Sue Stavenan, a high school teacher and homeowner in Plymouth, Minnesota, is the mother of two daughters, Kristina, age 6, and Katherine, age 2. She paid $140,000 to repair damage from the molds, to say nothing of the medical costs. She reported, "I started having problems with wheezing and sneezing when I visited the new house before we moved in . . . when I left it went away. I thought the house was just dirty." Then, after moving in, "The children got sick and never seemed to be well—at least as long as they were in the house. However, they were well away from home . . . but when they were back for awhile, they became lethargic, would wake up coughing and complain of stomachaches and sore throats."

Most of the homeowners surveyed in the *Star Tribune* series assumed that if they discovered defects in their new home, they would be able to get help from the builder, homeowners' insurance, home warranties—or perhaps as a last resort, the courts. But so far there has been no such help. They are left with anguish, frustration, a feeling of being abandoned, and a mountain of debt. After receiving a flood of phone calls from hundreds of homeowners, Senator John Marty and other Minnesota legislators proposed plans to change laws and regulations to make sure building codes are adequate and that owners have recourse if their houses have serious flaws. Similar efforts are being made in other states.

Sick Schools Syndrome

"Is Your School Sick?" This question, presented dramatically in a poster from the National Education Association (NEA), refers to another stressor that will become increasingly common in the next several decades. Several common problems can lead to the "sick school syndrome." These include:

- *Renovation Work:* As older school buildings are renovated, adults and students are exposed to volatile organic compounds (VOCs) in carpeting, tiles, and paint products.
- *Toxic Cleaning Substances and Art Supplies:* The markers in art classes and the chemicals in cleaning agents and floor waxes can contain toxic substances.
- *Other Chemicals and Fragrances:* Copy machine odors, science lab chemicals, air fresheners, perfumes, and other fragrances can add up to a total "stink."
- *Molds in Walls and Floors:* Water leakage from roofs and faulty gutters often set the stage for musty odors from mold growth.
- *Sealed Windows:* Energy-conserving windows and walls often serve as a barrier to fresh, clean air and can also limit ventilation.

20   These problems with our homes and schools are called the "Invisible Epidemic" by some observers, but they will become much more visible by the year 2000 and beyond.

Information resources are available for parents and teachers who are dealing with these "sick schools."

The NEA poster and a book, *Healthy School Handbook*, can be ordered by calling (800) 225-4200.

Doris Rapp, M.D., an environmental specialist from Buffalo, New York, has prepared an excellent video, "Environmentally Sick Schools." Call (800) 787-8780.

Booklets are available from the U.S. Environmental Protection Agency (EPA) at 401 M Street S.W., Washington, D.C. 20460.

Supplies and information catalog can be ordered from Environmental Health Shopper, P.O. Box 239, Fate, TX 75132.

Television and Children

The television sets in our homes also seem to provide "free lunch" in the form of free entertainment and free baby-sitting, but the problems of TV are *greater* than the benefits, according to researchers. Major movements are now afoot to rate TV programs and inform parents about content in programs. I witnessed the beginning of a positive and creative effort to deal with these problems—the kickoff of the Cornerstone Club at the Minneapolis Convention Center, sponsored by Aid Association for Lutherans (AAL) of Appleton, Wisconsin, and the National Institute on Media and the Family located in Minneapolis. Comedian Bill Cosby, along with John Gilbert, AAL president, David Walsh, president and founder of the National Institute on Media and the Family, and Colleen Needles, Twin Cities television personality, made excellent presentations to a large audience of parents, teachers, and interested citizens.

Dr. Walsh had recently finished a major study on the effects of television on violence and behavior problems in children. He reported these frightening facts about how children spend their time each week:

- ▨ Watching TV—24 hours
- ▨ Going to school—22 hours
- ▨ Time with mother—3.5 hours
- ▨ Time with father—30 minutes

Television has served as a baby-sitter and educator, but it is another lunch that is not free. Our society is now paying a huge price in youth and teen violence, truancy, addiction treatment, and medical and legal costs. Because of the great amount of time most children spend watching TV, the Institute has developed a unique KidScore to rate all programs. This is presented monthly in the magazine *Cornerstone*, which comes with membership in the Cornerstone Club. It also rates video games, which are so often filled with violence. The goal is to "stop the bad" and "use the good" in both TV and video games.

For further information, you may write: AAL Cornerstone Club, 4848 W. Converters Drive, Appleton, WI 54915-8008 or the National Institute on Media and the Family, 606 24th Avenue South, Suite 606, Minneapolis, MN 55454.

The Greenhouse Effect

My observations about the stresses I foresee as we look beyond A.D. 2000 would be incomplete without comments on the greenhouse effect, a result of our dependence on the free lunch of relatively inexpensive fossil fuels. The global warming that is predicted by international environmental observers is being discussed at the White House and the United Nations headquarters. It is too complex for most of us to understand fully, but a simplified explanation is that fuels like coal and oil make smoke

22   that acts like an extra blanket in the atmosphere. It traps heat from the sun and increases the planet's average surface temperature. Even a few degrees of increase will melt ice, raise sea levels, and swamp some coastal areas. It will also affect our forests, fisheries, and farms.

C. Ford Runge of the Department of Applied Economics and the College of Agriculture, Food and Environmental Sciences, University of Minnesota, has made this observation: "The key to reducing greenhouse house gas emissions without tying the economy in knots is to use market-based measures that recognize the importance of flexibility and innovation to control pollution at the lowest possible price . . . With just 4 percent of the world's population, the United States contributes nearly 25 percent of all man-made greenhouse emissions . . . The United States should welcome an international trading system to lower greenhouse gases. Properly developed and applied, it would transform the century's toughest environmental challenge with one of its most interesting economic opportunities."[6]

As the issues about global warming increase, President Clinton has pledged to "harness the power of the free market" for an assault on greenhouse gas pollution. His modest proposal, presented at the National Geographic Society in Washington, didn't please most industries or environmentalists, but it will help form the outline for international debate. Critics say his plan would not take effect until at least 2009, although the United States signed a treaty back in 1992 that requires a reduction in greenhouse gas emissions in the United States by the year 2000. European nations have argued for a stricter standard that would cut emissions to 15 percent less than 1990 levels by the year 2010. Yet, according to a review by *Time* magazine, the Department of Energy released a study one week prior to the announcement of the Clinton plan that showed emissions jumped 3.4 percent in 1996 alone.[7]

All of these trouble arrows increase the level of stress we
experience. Knowledge of these "free lunch" stressors can help
us understand our stress and manage it by defending ourselves
and building our reserve power. We will learn practical ways to
do this in Part Two.

WHAT'S NEW ABOUT STRESS?

3

If you ask, "What's new about stress?" the answer is, "Nearly everything." In this chapter I will focus on five of the most important breakthroughs involving stress: (1) heart disease, (2) chemical sensitivity, (3) delayed food allergies, (4) Candida-related complex (CRC), and (5) low serotonin levels.

Heart Disease and Stress

In an article in *Time* magazine entitled "Heart Disease: The Stress Connection," Dr. C. Noel Bairey Merz of Cedars-Sinai Medical Center in Los Angeles reported that 75 percent of the coronary patients tested demonstrated stress-triggered heart dysfunction that is ischemic, or related to low oxygen levels in the blood. The stressors identified in the study included such things as public speaking assignments, challenging mental arithmetic tasks, and psychological tests. An important finding was that most of these episodes were not accompanied by any obvious signs or symptoms noticeable by the patients. Dr. Merz said, "Thus, we were detecting a silent disease process."[1]

Another important discovery she made was that the most severe ischemia was found in individuals who had hostile and cynical outlooks on life. This finding was identified by the Hostility/Cynicism Questionnaire. (You may want to test yourself.)

Hostility/Cynicism Questionnaire

People make statements like those below from time to time in their daily lives. Based on how you feel today, answer true or false for each statement.

1. I have often had to take orders from someone who did not know as much as I did.
2. I think a great many people create a lot of their bad luck in order to gain the sympathy and help of others.
3. It takes a lot of argument to convince most people of the truth.
4. Most people are honest, mainly through fear of being caught.
5. Most people will use somewhat unfair means to gain profit or an advantage rather than lose it.
6. No one cares much what happens to you.
7. It is safer to trust nobody.
8. Most people make friends because friends are likely to be useful to them.
9. Inwardly most people do not like putting themselves out to help other people.
10. I have often met people who were supposed to be experts who were no better informed than I.
11. People often demand more respect for their own rights than they are willing to allow for the rights of others.
12. A large number of people are guilty of bad sexual behavior.
13. I think most people would lie to get ahead.

Add up all of your "True" responses. A score of two or less indicates that your hostility level is low; a score of three to six indicates your hostility level is of concern; a score of seven or greater indicates you have a high hostility level.

26   Dr. Merz went on to report on a large study in Canada aimed at developing stress management techniques for heart attack survivors. These techniques were used by nurses in the study and lowered the number of subsequent cardiac deaths by 51 percent. Nurses phoned patients monthly to rate stress levels and take action if levels were high. The program had a positive impact and reduced sudden and unexpected cardiac deaths. In another similar study, in addition to the telephone advice, patients were instructed in hatha yoga techniques, group support, low-fat diet, and regular exercise. These also helped reverse heart problems.

Other methods that have been found to be useful include contemplative prayer and meditation. Merz concluded her article by observing that if such programs are beneficial in patients with established heart disease, "it makes intuitive sense that similar beneficial effects should be seen in healthy subjects hoping to avoid heart disease."

Chemical/Environmental Sensitivity

If you were to ask Mary Lamielle, president of the National Center for Environmental Health Strategies (NCEHS), if multiple chemicals in the air we breathe are stressful, she would probably say, "Are you kidding? They sure are." Lamielle, founder and president of this patient advocacy group, calls for making the current ventilation recommendations of the American Society of Heating, Refrigeration and Air Conditioning Engineers (ASHRAE) a minimum national mandatory standard for all public and commercial buildings. She would also prohibit smoking in all public buildings. The NCEHS would also prohibit a number of products now used widely in public buildings: deodorizers that cause toxic or allergic reactions in some people, scents or perfumes that are used to affect the mood of occupants, and products (other than pesticides) that contain p-dichlorobenzene.

In excerpts from *Chemical and Engineering News,* Lamielle writes, "Many people with chemical sensitivity experience debilitating symptoms from deodorizing agents being pumped through building ventilation systems or spritzed into rooms." She would also like the EPA to develop product labeling for consumer products such as new carpets that emit volatile organic compounds (VOCs).[2]

When VOCs are released into the environment, they enter the human body via the air we breathe. Because they are long-chained chemical agents, our bodies are unable to detoxify or break them down. They then get stored in our body fat, our mucous surfaces, and our lymph tissues. In the toxic reactions that occur, the body is severely stressed. Scientists have known this at least since mustard gas was used in World War I to kill and injure enemy troops. Later, the Nazis used VOCs in the chambers of Buchenwald and other camps to exterminate imprisoned Jews.

The *Wall Street Journal* reports that more than one hundred Multiple Chemical Sensitivity (MCS) claims have been filed with the Equal Employment Opportunity Commission (EEOC) and are making their way through the courts. Already regulators and legal experts have established that patients with MCS can be classed as disabled under the Americans with Disabilities Act. David Sarvadi, a defense lawyer in Washington, D.C., says, "There is a lot of concern in the employer community about multiple chemical sensitivity under the Americans with Disabilities Act."[3] Listings of chemicals that pollute the air and cause stress range from auto and diesel exhaust to paint, varnish, lawn-care pesticides, and less obvious items such as odors from copy machines, correction fluid, and felt tip markers. More information is available from the National Center for Environmental Health Strategies (NCEHS), 1100 Rural Avenue, Vorhees, NJ 08043.

The Gulf War Syndrome, the subject of much controversy within the Department of Defense, the Veterans Administration,

28 and other federal authorities, is another example of chemical or environmental sensitivity. Troops in the Persian Gulf War were exposed to combinations of chemicals, including pesticides and nerve gases. Although passed off by some panelists as "postwar stress syndrome," the Gulf War Syndrome is much more serious than that, according to a study published in the *Journal of the American Medical Association*. Dr. Robert Haley of the University of Texas Southwestern Medical Center said, "The syndromes are due to subtle brain, spinal cord, and nerve damage . . . " Haley has identified three major symptom groups: (1) thought, memory, and sleep difficulties, (2) confusion, difficulty in reasoning, and occasional dizziness, (3) joint and muscle pain and tingling/numbness of hands and feet.[4]

Delayed Food Allergies/Sensitivities

There are two kinds of food allergies, *immediate* (IgE type) and *delayed* (IgG type). The classic immediate reaction occurs, for example, with an allergy to strawberries. There is an immediate rash of the face with itching that occurs within an hour or so. A common example of a delayed reaction would be allergies to dairy foods rich in the protein *casein*. Also, many people have delayed allergies to wheat and the protein *gluten* that is present in grains. The highest concentration of gluten is found in whole wheat products and the lowest in a grain called *spelt*, a grain often raised by Amish and Mennonite farmers. These foods cause delayed reactions much later, sometimes as long as twenty-fours hours after ingestion.

Over fifty medical conditions have now been associated with delayed food allergies. These include allergic rhinitis (nonseasonal runny nose), asthma, tinnitus (ringing of ears), headaches, hypoglycemia (low blood sugar), arthritis, Attention Deficit Disorder (ADD), eczema, gastrointestinal disorders (Crohn's disease, inflammatory bowel syndrome), insomnia,

obesity, irritability or anxiety symptoms, and even premenstrual
syndrome (PMS).

Many improvements in laboratory technology now make it possible to identify delayed food allergies. The most important method is called ELISA (Enzyme-Linked Immunosorbent Assay). It picks up IgG antibodies in more than one hundred common foods from a small blood sample. The ELISA test has been carefully standardized and its results have been evaluated by respected researchers such as Sidney Baker, M.D., formerly at Yale School of Medicine, and James Braly, M.D., author of *Dr. Braly's Food Allergy and Nutrition Revolution*. They estimate that more than 25 percent of individuals have one or more significant food allergies. The presence of such foods is stressful to the body.[5]

The test is not done by the usual hospital or clinic labs; samples are shipped to regional reference laboratories for analysis. One very reliable laboratory that I have used for several years is Immuno Laboratories in Fort Lauderdale, Florida. Interested persons can call (800) 231-9197 for more details and names of physicians in key cities across the nation who are familiar with the test.

Candida-Related Complex

An increasingly common cause of stress is, unfortunately, seldom treated and poorly understood by the majority of physicians in the United States. Indeed, when Christine Winderlin and I wrote our book *Candida-Related Complex* in 1996 we decided to subtitle it *What Your Doctor Might Be Missing*.[6] The reasons for this ignorance are unclear to me and the other physicians who have successfully treated the condition. A recent search by a former patient of mine, Dan Rogers, reported 5,820 citations in the medical literature.[7] F. C. Odds, a prominent British scientist, reported 6,000 references.[8]

30   Despite thousands of articles in scientific, medical, and popular magazines, the average doctor dismisses the problem.

CRC appears under many names, including *systemic candidiasis* and *dysbiosis*, or altered flora in the bowel, vagina, and elsewhere in the body. George Kroker, M.D., an allergist from La Crosse, Wisconsin, coined the name Candida-related complex (CRC).

CRC is caused by an overuse of antibiotics, which leads to infections by a microbe called *Candida albicans*. It is more than just a series of yeast infections. It also alters the immune system, causes emotional aberrations, such as depression and "brain fog," and exacerbates allergic responses to food and chemicals.

Surveying the nearly five thousand patients I have treated in the last ten years, I found that we had seen dramatic success with a program that included well-researched antifungals: Diflucan, Nizoral, and nystatin powder. Sugar is the favorite food of Candida, so CRC patients need to follow a low-sugar diet to starve the yeast. Add to this the liberal use of *Lactobacillus acidophilus*, preferably the brands that require refrigeration. These bacteria are the "good guys" we need in our digestive tract. When we take broad-spectrum antibiotics for, say, sore throat or bronchitis, the antibiotics kill these good guys along with the "bad guys," the strep or staph bacteria causing our illness. Then the normally present *Candida albicans* quickly overgrow and create multiple, complex symptoms.

A noted critic of the widespread overuse of antibiotics by the medical profession is Stephen Edelson, M.D., of the Environmental and Preventive Health Center in Atlanta. He also points out that yeast overgrowth is a stress producer. But antibiotics are not the only cause. As Dr. Edelson notes, "Then when you add the widespread use of antibiotics in animal feeds, which end up in our meats, high sugar in our diet and nutrient-poor foods in the American diet, many, many people develop chronic

Candida infections. The response to the body is toxic and stressful."[9] A good source of more information is U.A.S. Laboratories
(see Resources).

Low Serotonin Levels

An article that appeared in *Psychology Today* stated, "Stress does
not just grip us and let go. It changes us. It alters our bodies and
our brains!" New medical techniques have been developed to
measure mood-regulating hormones in the brain, such as serotonin, dopamine, and GABA, and to study their effects on our
emotions and moods.

The latest research from both Europe and the United
States shows that stress depletes the brain's "messenger service" by altering levels of these neurotransmitters. This can
cause disorders such as depression. Antidepressants such as
Prozac work by boosting serotonin levels. (More about alternative ways to increase serotonin in times of stress will be presented in chapter 17.)

How these hormones interrelate is shown in the figure on
the following page.

NORMAL STRESS OF DAILY LIVING

Every day we experience stress. "Stress does not just grip us and let us go. It changes us. It alters our bodies and our brains."

Psychology Today, Vol. 29, Jan./Feb. 1996

This chart will help you follow the complex response you experience EVERY time you encounter stress. A chain reaction begins and the Stress Cycle starts.

Causes Opioid Levels to Diminish
Creates a Sense of Urgency

LOWERED GABA

Feelings of anxiety, insecurity, unexplained panic, and depression are experienced.

INCREASED DOPAMINE

Feelings of alertness and anxiety rise. Emotional fatigue is created.

These feelings add to the Stress Cycle.

INCREASED NOREPINEPHERINE

Logic and deliberation diminish, creating an emotional response, anger, or hopelessness. Adrenaline is increased.

DECREASED SEROTONIN

This leads to poor sleep or insomnia. Lack of sleep creates irritability and a lack of rationality.

Your system is now in the "fight or flight" mode.

Causes opioid levels to decrease.

Oxygen and nutrients are diverted from vital organs to the muscles. Continued diversion starts the disease process. High blood pressure, stroke, heart attack, cancer, plus ...

Now the stress cycle builds upon itself.

THE STRESS CYCLE

An article by Rob Stein of the *Washington Post* states, "Researchers have long been puzzled by the fact that women are much more prone to certain mental health problems such as depression, eating disorders including anorexia, and schizophrenia."[10] Mirko Diksic, a neuroscientist at McGill University in Montreal, reports that serotonin levels differ between sexes. Since women produce less serotonin than men, it makes sense that they are more likely to have a shortage of this chemical under certain circumstances, such as stress. Whatever causes the stress, its physical effects are clear. When stress occurs, the "fight or flight response" begins. When confronted with a physical threat, our prehistoric ancestors learned to fight or run. Their bodies responded appropriately, with a surge of adrenaline. Their hearts beat faster and their muscles became stronger as blood was diverted to them from the digestive tract, skin, vital organs, and brain. Chemicals in their blood changed so that blood would clot quickly if there was an injury to the skin. Today we experience different types of stresses, such as bosses at work, kids at home, or traffic jams, but our physical responses to stress are the same. These responses can cause many ailments, including sleep disorders, weight problems, high blood pressure, gastrointestinal problems, asthma, and alcohol abuse.

I first started being aware of the chemical aberrations people can experience when I served as Medical Director of Health Recovery Center, an alcohol/chemical dependency clinic in Minneapolis. For years many experts in the dependency field have known that an addiction is not "all in your head." Psychological reasons alone do not account for alcoholism; it is more than drinking because we get upset or the boss is a bum or the spouse makes us nervous or the kids get on our nerves. Significantly low levels of serotonin are found among alcoholics, suggesting that drug and alcohol addiction is in part a response to chemical imbalance — an attempt to self-medicate.

34   In the book I wrote with Joan Mathews Larson, *Seven Weeks to Sobriety*, we noted that in 1972, Virginia Davis, a Texas researcher, found during autopsies of skid row alcoholics that their brains contained an opiate, which she mistook at first for heroin, but later found it to be an opiate-like compound she named THIQ (tetrahydroisoquiolines). These compounds or endorphins trick the brain into thinking the serotonin levels are normal—but, unfortunately, the alcoholic uses alcohol, which is highly toxic, instead of safe nutrients to make the serotonin. The alcohol-induced THIQs fasten onto the same receptor sites as the natural endorphins.[11]

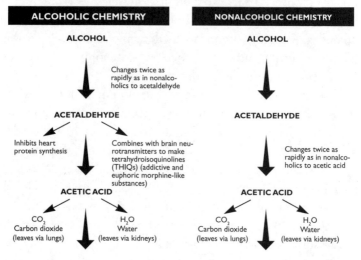

HOW THE BODY BREAKS DOWN ALCOHOL

These THIQs are present in alcoholics because they have a "genetic glitch" in the way they detoxify or break down alcohol. This genetic glitch is like other hereditary problems that set the stage in some families for conditions such as diabetes, cystic fibrosis, and hypothyroidism. Counseling and other traditional methods used in most alcohol/chemical dependency programs often fail over the long run to address this biochemical problem. Quality food and special nutrients such as amino acids, chromium, B-complex vitamins, and vitamin C have been shown to produce dramatic improvements (80 percent success) compared to the usual alcohol abstinence and counseling programs (20 percent success).[12]

I don't want to downplay programs like the Betty Ford Center in Palm Springs, California, and Hazelden in Center City, Minnesota, but I would advise them to explore more biochemical and nutritional options. I will give you some specific details in Part Two, where I will explain the concept that I call "Lake Serotonin," and suggest ways you can raise your serotonin levels as one way to manage your stress.

BIG-CITY STRESS

4

I seldom get sick, thank the Lord, but over the past several years, I have gotten sick in the "big city" and I would like to share some observations about what happened and why. It might help you better understand your stress and see why its causes are more than psychological.

I was raised in rural America, in Ellendale, North Dakota. I've also lived in the cities of Cleveland, Detroit, and Arlington, Virginia, a suburb of Washington, D.C. City living hasn't been bad most of the time, but I've become sick in about three days during trips to Los Angeles and New York City. Now if a healthy guy like me can get clobbered in three days, what about the citizens that live there for three years or three decades? Is it the stress of air pollution? Noise? Water quality? Radiation, or the impact of electromagnetic fields? Traffic? The food? Crime?

Dr. Bailus Walker Jr., professor of environmental and occupational toxicology at Howard University Cancer Center in Washington, D.C., said, "You've got to look at total exposure to everything that the body receives through the air, the food, the water. We can no longer look at these pieces in isolation. We've got to look at the total load!"[1] This is true for all of us, whether we live in big cities, suburbs, or small towns. In places like New York and Los Angeles I've felt all those "trouble arrows" aimed at me. In a recent trip to New York, for instance, I got off the plane at La Guardia Airport and here's what I experienced.

Environment

- ▨ *Noise*, including ambulance and fire sirens, honking horns and other sounds of traffic, the loud voices of truckers and teenagers shouting at each other.

- ▨ *Odors*, including diesel and auto exhaust and chemicals from factory smokestacks. In Los Angeles they are opening "oxygen bars." Actor Woody Harrelson is opening one in West Hollywood. For sixteen dollars customers will get twenty minutes of plain or fruit-scented oxygen. They will also be served health food and can have yoga sessions. According to an article in the *Los Angeles Times*, "Oxygen bars have become popular in Tokyo where the air is two to five times dirtier than in Los Angeles, which—despite its reputation—has improved its air quality."[2]

Lifestyle

- ▨ *Hurry*: Every other person on the street, especially on Broadway and Fifth Avenue, is running somewhere to get to an apartment or catch a taxi.

- ▨ *Smokers*: I've seen more smokers on the streets in New York City than anywhere else. Once you enter the restaurants, even in the no smoking sections, the smoke drifts your way and pollutes the air. On the positive side, there is a major campaign in New York City by SmokeFree Educational Services, phone: (212) 912-0960, which is working with Medallion Taxi Media to clean up the air. On many taxi-cabs you will see signs such as: "Virginia Slime: You've Come the Wrong Way, Baby!" Tobacco addiction is the number one cause of death and disease, killing 14,000 residents of New York City each year.

38 *Safety*

- ◩ *Traffic:* On several trips into New York I have had the frightening experience of nearly being sideswiped by angry truckers. And watch out for those taxi drivers hurtling down the street only to be stopped by another red light!
- ◩ *Crime:* Although the mayor of New York City says crime is down 10 percent, watch out!

Nutrition

- ◩ *Fast food* was invented in New York. Every other store has French fries, burgers, and snacks to eat on the run.
- ◩ *Fresh food:* It is hard to get fresh organic foods in many cities, and farmer's markets can be hard to find.

But that's enough bad stuff about the Big Apple. Let's move on—at a slow, stress-free pace, that is—to another Big City, my old stomping grounds of Washington, D.C., the home of my youngest daughter, Sarah.

Articles from magazines and the *Washington Post* tell about a new big-city stress called "road rage." It seems that the biggest hazard of our metropolitan streets is not the drunken driver, but the angry driver. A recent survey by the Washington metro area AAA showed that police and traffic reports find that 42 percent rated them as the greatest threat. Drunken drivers came in at 35 percent. In nearby Maryland, the study showed that traffic fatalities increased more than 33 percent from the previous year, and the state police concluded that many of the deaths were triggered by incidents of aggression and recklessness. Captain Grey Shipley of the Maryland State Police said, "Aggressive drivers operate with total disregard for the safety of others."

Richard Martinez, M.D., administrator of the National Highway Traffic Safety Administration says, "We have a new and growing problem called road rage. These drivers put themselves and others at risk by running stop signs and red lights, speeding, tailgating, weaving in and out of traffic, flashing their high beams, yelling, and making hostile hand and finger gestures. They treat other drivers—whom they've never met—like enemies."

Now what in the world is road rage? A good example was reported in the *Washington Post* under the headline "Drivers' Duel Blamed after 3 Die in GW Parkway Crash." The George Washington Memorial Parkway is a beautiful and scenic road on the west side of the Potomac River. The *Post* described how during the morning rush hour one driver, Bill Compe Jr., age twenty-six, was driving his Chevrolet Beretta to a construction job on Capitol Hill. The trouble began when another driver, Narkey Terry, also twenty-six years old and a computer technician, pulled in front of him with his red Jeep. Compe became angered and pulled out in front of Terry's Jeep.

The dueling then began. They chased each other for the next eight miles at speeds of up to eighty miles per hour. Suddenly, they ran across the median into oncoming traffic. There they hit two other cars in a terrible crash. Compe was killed, as were Nancy McBrian, age forty-one, a wife and mother of three, and George Smythe Jr., age forty-nine. Terry was injured but survived the accident and is now in prison serving a ten-year jail sentence. A review during his trial showed that at the time of the accident he was driving with a suspended license and had received fifteen traffic violations over the previous eight years!

With that snapshot of the current scene, let's talk history for a moment. More than one hundred years ago Horace Greeley, founder of the *New Yorker*, said, "Go west, young man, go west." (Today he would have to add, "young woman.") His advice was taken by thousands of families and west they went. That's where the gold, the silver, the great farmland, and the big forests were located. In more recent times—say, the last fifty years or so—the cry has been "Go to the big city." That is where the job opportunities, education, entertainment, and the lure of success have taken our young families and twenty-something

40   singles—cities like New York City, Los Angeles, Chicago, Denver, Washington, Cleveland, Detroit, Houston, Phoenix, Miami, or San Diego.

As with the westward movement, the urbanization of America hasn't been all "peaches and cream." Those who decided to go west to start a farm in Nebraska or pan for gold in California or start a business in Colorado experienced not only a lot of work but a lot of misery—bad weather, poor crops, disease, and other hardships. So it is with the young lawyer in Los Angeles who works eighty hours a week, the new schoolteacher in Washington, D.C., or the forty-something petroleum engineer in Houston—it's a tough and stressful life.

If you're one of the millions who live in or near our big cities, you are already experiencing these additional stressors. Even if you live in a small town or in the country, you are not immune to some of these environmental, lifestyle, safety, and nutritional problems. At the least, the TV, radio, and Internet can bring them all into your home.

By being more aware of these stressors and understanding their effects on us, we can learn to better manage our own stress and that of our loved ones.

THE STRESS OF
BEING OVERWEIGHT

You've seen TV programs about it. You've heard about it on your car radio while driving home from work. Nearly every magazine and newspaper editor decided it was newsworthy enough for front-cover or front-page articles. Even former U.S. Surgeon General C. Everett Koop heard about it and got so angry he decided to "declare war on obesity." You've also read about the reasons behind the Food and Drug Administration (FDA) actions that pulled Redux and fenfluramine off the market and left hundreds of thousands of patients and thousands of physicians scratching their heads in confusion and bewilderment. What should a person do? What is the uproar all about?

The reason for the uproar was the statistic that more than one-third (33.4 percent) of all adults in the United States are now overweight—or even worse "obese" (I'll explain that word later). With that problem come significant health hazards. These include hypertension, cardiovascular disease (heart attack, poor circulation, and type II diabetes), and other problems such as high cholesterol, sleep apnea, and even infertility.

Adding to the stress of overweight citizens is that their spouse, parent, friend, and fellow worker have also heard the news and are showing them the clippings and articles. Years before it became front-page news, these overweight Americans heard about it from schoolmates who called them "Fats" or "Fatty" or used the nursery rhyme "Fatty, fatty, two by four . . ." Later on, friends commented, "You never got back to normal

42   after that second baby, did you?" or a spouse observed, "You'd
      better lose a few pounds before you go to the class reunion" or
      "Your feet wouldn't hurt if you lost thirty pounds."

      Afflicted women note a gradual increase in dress size until
      they get to size 14 or 16. They notice their waist has scooted up
      to thirty-eight inches and their hips up to forty. Afflicted men
      see belt sizes jump to forty-six inches instead of the thirty-four
      they had in the army or navy. Someone might say, "You've got a
      'beer belly' now, Fred!" even though he didn't drink beer at all.
      For all it is a time of frustration and soul-searching. With the
      frustration comes stress, hypoglycemia (low blood sugar), more
      snacking, and more calories.

      Out of this frustration comes an effort to find out why peo-
      ple become overweight—or worse, obese. Is it because they
      are couch potatoes? Is it a hormone problem like hypothy-
      roidism? In women is it estrogen? Does hypoglycemia result
      from too much insulin (hyperinsulinemia)? Is it because the
      American diet is loaded with sugar and carbohydrates? Is it just
      in the genes?

      The answer to many of these questions is yes. But research
      is turning up even more possibilities, adding at least one to the
      list of questions: "Is being overweight caused by stress?" Some of
      this new information comes from studies in Sweden by Dr. Per
      Bjorntorp in Göteborg. He and his associates have shown that
      stress, along with related anxiety and depression, increases the
      accumulation of visceral or abdominal fat. Apparently, stress
      triggers the "fight or flight reaction" and stimulates the adrenal
      glands to go into high gear, producing adrenaline and cortisol
      and making fat deposits in the process. A recent article by Dr.
      Bjorntorp concludes with this statement: "This again suggests
      the need for stress management may be more critical, or as crit-
      ical, as [traditional] weight loss treatment."[1]

      These Swedish findings are consistent with my work in the
      treatment of weight-loss patients. Time and again I've heard
      these insights:

"It was the divorce that did it to me."
"I never had trouble until Mom died, and now I'm taking care of Dad with his Alzheimer's."
"It was all that darned travel I did for the company. I was off to New York or Chicago or L.A. nearly every week."
"I did well until the Christmas holidays. Then I was so busy that I had to drop out of the program — and I'm back to 210 pounds. Stress did it again."

Earlier in this chapter, I promised to explain the word *obese*. This medical term means more than being overweight. The best definitions and insight come from the American Society of Bariatric Physicians (ASBP) and the American Obesity Association (AOA). The members of ASBP (I'm one) are physicians who specialize in the treatment of obesity and weight problems. Their treatment is based on the Body Mass Index (BMI), which is calculated by taking the patient's weight in kilograms and dividing it by their height in meters squared. This complicated math is done with the aid of a fat analyzer or scale. A popular brand that I have used is the Tanita scale (see Resources), which gives a digital readout. Measurements are done at intervals of four weeks to ascertain progress. (See chapter 14 for an easy way to determine your BMI.) If the BMI is 27 (or above), the patient qualifies for the adjective "obese."

In a recent article in the *American Journal of Bariatric Physicians*, Richard L. Atkinson, M.D., president of the AOA, described the four levels he uses in looking at BMI:[2]

1. Minimal and Low Risk: BMI rating of 25 or less. Physician suggests attention to diet, increased activity, and lifestyle changes.

2. Moderate: BMI rating of 27–30. Same suggestions as above plus low-calorie diet (800–1,200 calories per day).

3. High and Very High: BMI rating of 30–40. Same suggestions as above plus drug therapy and very low-calorie diet (less than 800 calories per day). If medication is to be used,

certain other medical factors must be reviewed when the BMI is 27 or more.

4. Extremely High: BMI rating of 40 or more. Same suggestions as above plus option for surgery. Here the term *option for surgery* includes these procedures: Jejunoileal bypass, vertical banded gastroplasty, gastric bypass, and partial biliopancreatic bypass.[3] These are all complicated surgical procedures that only a few specialists perform.

There is also new scientific information about the role of serotonin in regulating weight. Serotonin has a neurochemical role that is the opposite of dopamine, another neurotransmitter. Both serve many functions throughout the body, including regulating things like body temperature, appetite, mood, thirst, and cravings. Dopamine and serotonin shortages and imbalances cause various symptoms, including weight change. When serotonin levels are too low, there are more hungry spells and people tend to eat more. In an excellent article in *Time* called "The Mood Molecule," a professor from Northwestern University, James Stockard, describes serotonin in a poetic way: "A person's mood is like a symphony, and serotonin is like the conductor's baton."[4]

The evidence is now overwhelming that, like hypertension or other cardiovascular disease or diabetes, obesity is a complex metabolic disorder that involves multiple organs and endocrine systems. But a recent survey found that most doctors don't treat obesity unless the patient is already significantly overweight. Even then, according to the same study, most family physicians, internists, and endocrinologists intervene with only 50 percent of such patients. Other specialists report intervening with only 5 to 29 percent of these individuals.[5] The reasons for this are unclear, but I have observed that many physicians and patients are uncertain about what they can and should be doing. There are fears and confusion about medications, diets, and procedures. Many physicians are skeptical about weight-management programs because of the "yo-yo" experience: so many people, including celebrities such as Oprah Winfrey, have tried various weight-loss methods only to regain the weight in the next six months.

Dr. Koop has said, "Physicians can no longer sit on the sidelines as America's obesity epidemic reaches crisis levels . . . physicians have completely overlooked weight maintenance as a disease prevention strategy."[6] Koop and other physicians have developed guidelines for doctors and patients. They are available for three dollars by writing to: Shape Up America! 6707 Democracy Blvd., Suite 107, Bethesda, MD 20817. Many other resources for weight problems are available now through health-food stores and many weight-loss clinics. Some of them are described in chapter 14, where you also will find my Ten Commandments for maintaining your proper weight. For a list of physicians who are experts in the treatment of obesity, write: American Society of Bariatric Physicians, 5600 S. Quebec Street, Suite 109, Englewood, CO 80111.

With the help of Dr. Koop, the American Obesity Association, the American Society of Bariatric Physicians, and researchers in the United States, Sweden, and elsewhere, progress is being made in the attitudes of physicians, patients, and the public in general regarding obesity. Many now recognize it as a metabolic disorder. It is not just "pill stuff" to be treated with prescriptions, nor is it just "talk stuff" to be treated with counseling or pep talks. It does not require merely calorie counting or more exercise. It involves all of the above plus a better understanding of stress. Experts agree that stress is a cause, and stress management is an essential part of treatment.

6 THE STRESS OF GROWING OLDER

It's been called "The Graying of America." More of us are living longer than ever before. For the first time in our history many people are reaching age sixty-five who can look forward to twenty years or more of healthy, productive living. The downside is that there are additional stresses to growing old—stresses related to the inevitable changes and losses we all experience in those years.

Of course, all of us are aging day by day. Even though you may now be in your twenties or forties, you will almost certainly face the stresses associated with aging. You will be able to manage these stresses better if you understand what happens as we age and take steps to live well now in preparation for being an "elder." If you are already among the elders of our society, you can maximize these bonus years.

Recently I read Scott Walker's book *Glimpses of God*, in which he wrote about the struggles of adult years, the challenges of marriage, the intoxication of success, and the fear of failure. But the phrase that really grabbed me was "the creeping awareness of mortality." Walker contends that this awareness "causes us to reach out for strength and power beyond ourselves. Only then are we ready to discover the Holy Spirit of God and the wheel of the universe on which all else revolves."[1]

I might have overlooked this passage as I read it except that several things had happened the same week to make me receptive: (1) I had just celebrated my birthday with family and friends; (2) I had recently closed my clinical office and retired after forty-two years of medical work; and (3) I had spent an enjoyable Memorial Day with two of my four grandchildren and their parents. With these events began my own awareness of mortality. I asked myself hard questions like: "Will I live to see my grandchildren graduate from high school?" "Will they need my financial help for college?" "How can they survive the pitfalls of violence and amorality so common with teenagers these days?" "What can I do to help them become good Christians?" Then, as if these thoughts weren't profound enough for me, I picked up the morning paper and happened to read the obituary page. One glance showed that 50 percent of those listed were younger than me. More stress!

At about that time my wife and I were invited to a special event at Jones Harrison Residence, an assisted living and nursing home facility that is now the home of Colleen's mother. As we entered the front door, strolled in, and looked for the right way to the event, we were caught up in a traffic jam of wheelchairs and walkers. It made this visitor think, "Is this where I'll be in five or ten years?" Thoughts like that are also downright stressful.

Then I decided I needed a heavy dose of prayer and advice, so I read more of what Walker had to say. He wrote, "In a way we are like the television set without an antenna. Just as television waves filled the room that night, so the Spirit of God always surrounds us, infiltrating our total being. Yet, for some reason, we are unable to tune in and receive God's strength, peace, joy, and vitality. Our TV picture of the world remains fuzzy and our perspective of reality becomes distorted. God's voice is muffled. How can we change our situation and be empowered by God's Spirit? . . . How can we fashion our own spiritual antenna and get back in touch with God?"[2]

That's the challenge. That's the goal.

When my antenna gets a little loose from everyday stress and I get a little down, that's when I get the most from attending church. Hearing the organ . . . singing with the choir . . .

48 watching the little kids go up in front for the children's sermon . . . listening to the pastor . . . going to the coffee hour to chat with friends—these lift my spirit and help me collect my thoughts. One of my favorite poets, Henry Wadsworth Longfellow, said it well when he wrote:

> Lives of great men all remind us,
> We can make our lives sublime,
> And departing leave behind us,
> Footprints in the sand of time.

This poem makes me reflect:

- What are my lasting footprints?
- Did I make a difference for my spouse, my kids?
- Did I make a difference in my job, my profession, my career, my community?
- What will my obituary state?
- Is there someone I should say thanks to that I've been too busy to respond to for helping me, teaching me, advising me, or giving me a job?
- Is there someone I should make amends with for a past oversight or transgression?
- Can I offer personal or financial help to some needy person who needs a lift—or a nudge?
- Should I spend more time meditating and praying about seeking the Lord's help?

A book I helped write with Tamora Mahnerd, *Keys to a New Life: Psychological and Biochemical Insights about Weight Loss*, contains this statement: "Changes occur naturally over time with our bodies. The aging process brings with it certain changes . . . These are natural and to resist them and consider them as negative is unwise. Each body has its own combination of qualities that fit together perfectly."[3]

A special issue of *U.S. News and World Report* included a feature entitled "How Time Takes Its Toll." The article begins:

"Even if you're already forty or fifty, it could be decades before you fully realize you're aging. The loss of 40 percent of lung capacity by age eighty, say, is so gradual that most people never sense the difference. And the signposts of aging depend partly on the individual. As car people say, your mileage may vary."[4] But each decade has its own signposts. There are a few generalities we can make about the aging process, which may help in learning how to recognize the stresses we face before they get to be too much.

Your Forties

At forty, the body burns 120 fewer calories a day than at age thirty, making weight control harder. One reason for this is that people in their forties tend to be more sedentary in their jobs, family activities, and social life. This can be overcome with regular exercise—the vigorous kind involving jogging, biking, or walking. But to that regimen must be added "friendly detours" such as walking up the steps instead of using the elevator or escalator. When you go to church, don't park in the lot next to the church; park a block away and walk. When you go to the store, don't park at the nearest exit; walk further. When you need to mail a letter, walk to the postbox; don't leave it in the mail slot for the mail carrier to pick up.

The body is five-eighths of an inch shorter at forty than at thirty, and it will continue to shrink by about one-eighteenth of an inch each year because of bone loss, changes in posture, and compression of the spongy discs that separate the vertebrae. Some of the changes in the disc and the joints can be minimized by regular stretching exercises for the back and spine. (See chapter 16 for unstress exercises.)

Changes in the inner ear erode the ability to hear higher frequencies, especially for men, who lose hearing more than twice as fast as women do. The eyes also begin to have trouble

50   focusing on magazines and other close objects as the lenses become thicker.

Your Fifties

With menopause, fertility ends and lower estrogen speeds bone loss and raises the risk of heart disease. Many of the risks of heart disease and arteriosclerosis can be minimized with the addition of vitamin B_6, B_{12}, and folic acid, as pointed out by Dr. Kilmer S. McCully in his book *The Homocysteine Revolution.* (Keats Publishing, New Canaan, Connecticut).

As the eye's sensitivity to contrast declines, so diminishes the ability to see in dim light or under conditions of glare and to see moving objects clearly. Loss of strength becomes measurable as muscle mass diminishes. This can be minimized by doing simple exercises such as push-ups, deep knee bends, biceps flexing, and walking, jogging, swimming, or biking regularly and vigorously.

Vulnerability to infections and cancer increases; the thymus, a gland that plays a key role in the immune system, has shrunk by 90 to 95 percent. Vulnerability to infections can be decreased by taking more vitamin C—take the capsules, not the chewables—in doses of 2,000 mg a day. Add to that 400 units of vitamin E, 10,000 units of vitamin A, and a good multivitamin/mineral tablet or capsule each morning.

Your Sixties

As high-frequency hearing deteriorates further, following conversations becomes harder, especially for men, since consonants, which carry most of the meaning of speech, largely consist of higher frequencies. With that sort of loss be extra careful of all loud noises, such as that of the snowblower and lawn mower. Avoid them, if possible, by hiring someone to do the work.

The pancreas, which processes glucose, works less efficiently by this time. Blood-sugar levels rise, and more people are diagnosed with adult-onset diabetes. Taking a 20 mcg tablet of chromium picolinate every morning can often lower chances of adult-onset diabetes. If you have a history of diabetes in older members of your family, start the chromium in your forties or fifties. It helps the islets of Langerhans in your pancreas make a better amount of insulin.

Joints are stiff in the morning, particularly the knees, hips, and spine, because of wear and tear on the cartilage that cushions them. Taking a product called glucosamine sulfate gives good results by helping the cartilage "cushions" stay "glued" to the bone. I recommend two 750 mg capsules at breakfast. Knees, hips, and spine will say "thanks." (See Resources.)

Men's sexual daydreams all but vanish after age sixty-five. Researchers don't know why.

Your Seventies

Blood pressure is 20 to 25 percent higher than in the twenties; the thicker, stiffer artery walls can't flex as much with each heartbeat. More than half of men in their seventies show signs of coronary-artery disease. You've heard it a million times, but I'll say it one more time—Exercise! It keeps the arteries more elastic. Jog or play tennis or do your favorite exercise—like walking, biking, or swimming—and add a supplement like CardioHelper; I recommend two capsules per day. It helps keep the homocysteine levels down. (See Resources.)

Reaction to loud noises and other stimuli is delayed as the brain's ability to send messages to the extremities slows. Sweat glands shrink or stop working in both men and women, raising the risk of heatstroke (but reducing the need for deodorant). Short-term memory and the ability to learn spoken material, such as a new language, decline with changes in brain function.

52   This problem, so common to many of us well before our seventies, now has a variety of treatments. The Chinese have used ginkgo biloba for many centuries. Studies in the United States shows it helps people with Alzheimer's to function better. It helps improve the blood flow to the brain, improves cognitive (memory) functions, and inhibits platelet dysfunctions that increase the risk of blood clots in the brain and elsewhere. It comes in 60 mg capsules with a dosage of one to three per day. (See Resources.)

Your Eighties

Women in their eighties become particularly susceptible to falls that can cause disabling hip fractures. They are generally weaker than men and by now many have lost more than half the bone mass in the hips and upper legs.

Almost half of those over eighty-five show signs of Alzheimer's disease. The heart beats, at maximum exertion, about 25 percent slower than it did at age twenty—but compensates by expanding and pumping more blood per beat.

The stereotype notwithstanding, personality doesn't change with age. A cranky eighty-year-old was a cranky thirty-year-old.

So, yes, our bodies do change as we get older. Yes, the gray hair, the baldness, the arthritic knee, the trouble remembering names do create stress. The complexities of wills and estate planning and trusts create stress. The visits to the doctor or hospital create stress. The loss of spouses and dear friends creates stress. So what words of wisdom can a family doctor, author, spouse, father, grandfather say to counteract the stresses noted above?

As I was pondering these issues, I read a wall hanging given to my wife on Mother's Day. Although obviously meant for children, the advice was so good I said, "That's wisdom also for senior citizens"—and all of us.

Be an Angel

Share your favorite things with others.
Keep your halo polished.
Show respect for older people.
Always mind your manners.
Make friends with someone who is shy.
Plant a garden for butterflies.
Say at least one nice thing to someone everyday.
Never make fun of anyone.
Make your bed every morning.
Talk to plants to help them grow.
Think happy thoughts.
Don't make too much noise when you flap your wings.
Clean up after yourself and clean up after others.
Donate part of your allowance to a worthy cause.
Always tell the truth.
Be patient with those who don't fly as fast as you do.
Sprinkle a little stardust wherever you go.

7 DON'T BE AFRAID TO TAKE THREE MORE TESTS

Now that you've read about the new stresses that might be inhabiting your stress-filled world, it's time to apply this knowledge to yourself and evaluate further your own stress level. The following three quizzes will help you gain valuable insights into managing your own stress:

1. How Vulnerable Are You to Stress?

2. Self-Test for Type A Personality

3. Self-Test for Stress Levels

After you've finished each test and given yourself a score, I'll explain what your score means.

How Vulnerable Are You to Stress?

This test was developed at Boston University by Lyle H. Miller and Alma Dell Smith. They point out that each of us has warning signals when it comes to stress. Some people get headaches as their signal. Others get indigestion and acid stomach; others suffer from insomnia.

Score each item from 1 for "almost always" to 5 for "never," according to how much of the time each statement applies to you.

___ 1. I eat at least one hot, balanced meal a day.

___ 2. I get seven to eight hours sleep at least four nights a week.

___ 3. I give and receive affection regularly.

___ 4. I have at least one relative within fifty miles on whom I can rely.

___ 5. I exercise to the point of perspiration at least twice a week.

___ 6. I smoke less than half a pack of cigarettes a day.

___ 7. I drink fewer than five alcoholic drinks a week.

___ 8. I am the appropriate weight for my height.

___ 9. I have an income adequate to meet basic expenses.

___10. I get strength from my religious beliefs.

___11. I regularly attend club or social activities.

___12. I have a network of friends and acquaintances.

___13. I have one or more friends to confide in about personal matters.

___14. I am in good health (including eyesight, hearing, teeth).

___15. I am able to speak openly about my feelings when angry or worried.

___16. I have regular conversations with the people I live with about domestic problems, such as chores, money, and other daily living issues.

___17. I do something fun at least once a week.

___18. I am able to organize my time effectively.

___19. I drink fewer than three caffeinated drinks (coffee, tea, cola) a day.

___20. I take quiet time for myself during the day.

___TOTAL

After you've marked your scores, add the figures up and then subtract twenty. Any number over thirty indicates a vulnerability to stress. If the score is between fifty and seventy-five you are getting into the "danger zone." If it's over seventy-five, you need to take swift action to avoid disaster.

56 *Self-Test for Type A Personality*

Type A persons are our hard-driving, overly conscientious, high-achieving friends, neighbors, and coworkers. Recent studies have also shown they are more likely to be hostile or cynical. They are perfectionists living in an imperfect world. That frequently makes them angry—at bosses, spouses, or fellow workers. That is probably why there are more heart attacks on Monday morning than any other time in the week! On the other end of the spectrum are Type B people, who are more laid-back and easygoing. Stress, whether big or small, always bothers the Type A the most and the Type B the least.

As you can see, each item below is composed of a pair of adjectives or phrases separated by a series of numbers (1 through 7). Each pair represents two kinds of contrasting behavior. Each of us belongs somewhere along the line between these two extremes; most of us are neither the most competitive nor the least competitive person we know. Circle the number where you think you belong between the two extremes.

Add together the value of all the numbers you have circled for your total score.

1.	Doesn't mind leaving things temporarily unfinished	1 2 3 4 5 6 7	Must finish things once started
2.	Calm and unhurried about appointments	1 2 3 4 5 6 7	Never late for appointments
3.	Not competitive	1 2 3 4 5 6 7	Highly competitive
4.	Listens well, lets others finish speaking	1 2 3 4 5 6 7	Anticipates others in conversation (interrupts, finishes others' sentences)
5.	Never in a hurry, even when pressured	1 2 3 4 5 6 7	Always in a hurry
6.	Able to wait calmly	1 2 3 4 5 6 7	Uneasy when waiting
7.	Easygoing	1 2 3 4 5 6 7	Always going full speed ahead
8.	Takes one thing at a time	1 2 3 4 5 6 7	Tries to do more than one thing at a time, thinks about what to do next

9.	Slow and deliberate in speech	1 2 3 4 5 6 7	Vigorous and forceful in speech (uses a lot of gestures)
10.	Concerned with satisfying self, not others	1 2 3 4 5 6 7	Wants recognition by others for a job well done
11.	Does things slowly	1 2 3 4 5 6 7	Does things quickly (eating, walking, etc.)
12.	Easygoing	1 2 3 4 5 6 7	Hard-driving
13.	Expresses feelings openly	1 2 3 4 5 6 7	Holds feelings in
14.	Large number of interests	1 2 3 4 5 6 7	Few interests outside work
15.	Satisfied with job	1 2 3 4 5 6 7	Ambitious, desires quick professional advancement
16.	Never sets own deadlines	1 2 3 4 5 6 7	Often sets own deadlines
17.	Feels limited responsibility	1 2 3 4 5 6 7	Always feels responsible
18.	Never judges things in terms of numbers	1 2 3 4 5 6 7	Often judges performance in terms of numbers (how many, how much)
19.	Casual about work	1 2 3 4 5 6 7	Takes work very seriously
20.	Not very precise	1 2 3 4 5 6 7	Very precise (careful about detail)

Total score = 110 to 140: Type A_1

If you are in this category, you are likely to have a high risk of developing cardiac illness, especially if you are over forty and smoke.

Total score = 80 to 109: Type A_2

You are in the direction of being cardiac prone, but your risk is not as high as the A_1. Nevertheless, you should pay careful attention to the advice given to all Type As.

Total score = 60 to 79: Type AB

You are a mixture of A and B patters. This is a healthier pattern than either A_1 or A_2, but you have the potential for slipping into A behavior and should recognize this.

Total score = 30 to 59: Type B_2

Your behavior is on the less cardiac-prone end of the spectrum. You are generally relaxed and cope adequately with stress.

Total score = 0 to 29: Type B_1

You tend to the extreme of noncardiac traits. Your behavior expresses few of the reactions associated with cardiac disease.

58   *Self-Test for Stress Levels*

An integral part of my clinical assessment for the past sixteen years has been the "Self-Test for Stress Levels" developed by Thomas Homes and Richard Rahe at the University of Washington's School of Medicine. It measures the stressful events in your life.

Instructions: Circle the items that have applied to you within the last twelve months. Enter your total at the bottom.

Life Event   Value

 1. Death of spouse 100
 2. Divorce 73
 3. Marital separation.............................. 65
 4. Jail term 63
 5. Death of close family member.................... 63
 6. Personal injury or illness....................... 53
 7. Marriage 50
 8. Fired at work................................... 47
 9. Marital reconciliation........................... 45
10. Retirement 45
11. Change in health of family member 44
12. Pregnancy...................................... 40
13. Sexual difficulties 39
14. New family member............................. 39
15. Business readjustment 39
16. Change in financial status 38
17. Death of a close friend 37
18. Change to a different profession 36
19. Change in the number of arguments with spouse..... 35
20. Mortgage over $100,000........................ 31
21. Foreclosure of mortgage or loan.................. 30
22. Change in responsibilities at work................ 29
23. Son or daughter leaving home.................... 29

24. Trouble with in-laws 29
25. Outstanding personal achievement 28
26. Spouse begins or stops work 26
27. Begin or end school 26
28. Change in living conditions 25
29. Revision of personal habits 24
30. Trouble with boss 23
31. Change in work hours or conditions 20
32. Change in residence 20
33. Change in schools 20
34. Change in recreation 19
35. Change in church activities 19
36. Change in social activities 18
37. Mortgage or loan of less than $100,000 17
38. Change in number of family get-togethers 15
39. Change in sleeping habits 15
40. Change in eating habits 15
41. Single person living alone . . . . *
42. Other—describe . . . . *
43. Other—describe . . . . *

TOTAL ____

*Give appropriate points yourself

If your combined score is over 150, it's been a bad year. If it's over 200, it has been a terrible year, and there is increased risk for health problems.

You have taken some important steps in learning to manage your own stress. You have gained more understanding of the trouble arrows that bombard us every day—especially the new environmental stressors. The self-tests have made you more aware of your own stress levels and the risks you face.

Now you're ready for Part Two, where you will learn five ways to manage your stress and practical steps you can take to defend yourself from trouble arrows and build your reserve power.

PART TWO:
MANAGING
STRESS

8 | FIVE STEPS TO MANAGE STRESS

Stress management is a puzzle. Why does one life event cause minor distress to one individual and wreak havoc on another? This kind of discrepancy can mystify doctors and counselors, as well as the family and friends involved. My fellow physicians are often reluctant to help solve the puzzle and so take the easy way out: "I'm sorry about what happened. Here's a prescription that might help. Take two to four tablets a day."

You have by now taken the three tests in chapter 7. Maybe your scores were high—even in the "danger zone," or at least higher than you expected. So what do you do next?

Start with these five ways to manage stress:

Step 1: Regain Control of Your Life
Step 2: Learn How to Relax
Step 3: Nourish Your Body
Step 4: Exercise Away Stress
Step 5: Care for Your Spirit

Persons with good health, successful relationships, and meaningful careers all know that the best way to manage stress is to be holistic. This means taking care not only of the body and mind, but also of the spirit. Worship, prayer, and meditation are integral parts of any program of stress management.

Also, as you delve into these five ways, remember the ABLE acronym: Accept more individual responsibility for health of self and family; Become wise buyers and intelligent users of health-care services, medications, supplements, and nutritional

64   options; Learn skills of observation and identification of everyday ills and injuries, learn the meaning of symptoms, and, with
proper guidance, develop self-confidence regarding health
issues; Educate others about health attitudes, stress management, self-care, exercise, and environmental issues in order to
improve your community's health in general.

I want you to especially remember *Educate*. After you have
learned these skills you must—and I emphasize must—educate
others. Tell your kids, spouse, fellow workers, friends at church,
and neighbors what you have learned. By telling another person, you really learn. Ask any teacher or any lecturer who has
prepared a speech for a special class or event. Who learns more
than the student in the process? You do!

Step 1
Regain Control of Your Life

9 SETTING BOUNDARIES AT HOME AND WORK

As a family doctor and stress expert, I have advised many patients over the past four decades to set limits on their daily duties at home and work, to "Just say no!" to some of the many demands on their time and resources. When I read the excellent book *Boundaries: When to Say Yes and When to Say No to Take Control of Your Life* by Henry Cloud and John Townsend, I discovered I wasn't the only doctor giving this sort of advice.[1] These authors are clinical psychologists at the Minirth-Meier Clinic West, headquartered in Newport Beach, California, and specialize in the integration of Scripture and psychology. The book offers useful tips about how to set healthy boundaries with spouses, parents, children, friends, and coworkers.

At the beginning of the book, Drs. Cloud and Townsend describe the toils and troubles of Sherrie, a working mom, her husband, Walt, their nine-year-old son, Todd, and six-year-old daughter, Amy. The family's day begins at 6:45 when Sherrie's alarm goes off and she begins ticking off her day's schedule.

As she washes her face she ponders: "Let's see: fix breakfast, pack two lunches, finish sewing Amy's costume for the school play; that will be a trick finishing sewing the costume before my car pool picks me up at 7:45 A.M.!"

Still bleary-eyed from too little sleep the night before, she also begins thinking about the 4:30 meeting with Todd's third grade teacher, who phoned Sherrie earlier that week because of Todd's recent behavior problems at school. After gulping down some toast and juice, it is time for the sewing job she meant to do last night but was interrupted by a visit from her mother. Although a widow for twelve years, Sherrie's mother has elevated widowhood to martyrdom. When she arrived the night before, she said with a long, sad face, "I'd be the last to intrude on your time with your family, but since your father died, it's been such an empty time."

By the time her mother left there was no time for the school costume, and Sherrie collapsed into bed at 11:30 P.M. So here it was, "deadline time" and "I've got to get that costume done before my ride gets here." She arrived at work a little late and the meeting had already started. Every eye was on her as she struggled into her seat. Sherrie knew it was going to be "a bad day." She managed to leave early for the 4:30 teacher/parent conference regarding her son's inappropriate behavior. Was he hyperactive? Was she guilty of bad parenting?

The teacher made some good recommendations, and by 5:15 P.M. Sherrie was driving home from school and mulling over what to fix for dinner . . . what time she had to be at church for the committee meeting . . . how to get ready for her new work assignment at the office . . . how she could persuade her husband, Walt, not to ask his friends over to watch the football game on Saturday . . . etc.

After supper she asked herself over and over, "What am I doing to myself? I'm overwhelmed! When should I stop? Where do I draw the line?"

The evening whizzed by and, before she knew it, it was 11:50 P.M. With a mixture of fatigue and anxiety she picked up her Bible, which was open to Matthew 5:3-5 and read, "Blessed are the poor in spirit, for theirs is the kingdom of heaven. Blessed are those who mourn, for they shall be comforted. . . . "

Sherrie paused for a minute and then prayed, "But, Lord, I already feel poor in spirit. I mourn over my life, my marriage, my children. I try to be gentle, but I just feel run-over all the time. . . . Dear Lord, what am I to do?"[2]

68   That is the million-dollar question that thousands of "Sherries" across the nation are asking themselves. They may have poor sleep, anxiety, and more illness than normal. They feel rotten. When they pick up *People* magazine or their hometown newspaper, they see ads for a popular drug to lessen anxiety. They wonder if their doctor could give them the "magic pill." Should they see a psychologist or a psychiatrist for advice? Should they go to a support group at church? What is the best solution?

First, we should look at what we mean by boundaries. Homeowners and business owners know about property boundaries. They know about fences, walks, hedges, and "No Trespassing" signs. They know that owners are legally responsible for what happens on their property regarding kids, dogs, cats, noise, lawn chemicals, and the accidents that might happen there. You can go to the county courthouse and look at the plats and see where the property lines are actually located.

But what about property lines and boundaries on a personal level? What is "me" and what is "not me"? Where are the limits and boundaries where "me" ends and "someone else" begins? When you are in control of your life emotionally and physically, you can set boundaries that work. It may be difficult, and it may take some experimentation, but follow your wisdom and you will learn as you go. Here are a few tips to get you started.

- Do one thing at a time. Focus only on what you do. Do not look back or ahead while you are working. Live in the now.
- Do the best you can, and let go of worry about the outcome. You have done your best.
- Let go of worry about things over which you have no control. Such worry is useless and self-destructive.
- If you feel closed in, look for alternative choices. Realize that there are always options in anything you have to do.
- Recognize your own limitations, and within those boundaries set realistic goals for yourself.

- When a crisis occurs, face it. Take constructive action and organize a proper response. Be flexible.
- Be active and productive.

You can set boundaries in your private life when things are stressful and out of control. Here are some tips for defining them:

- Learn to say no.
- Remember, even when others ask for your help you sometimes have to draw the line. While service and giving are important parts of healthy life, being unable to assert yourself and claim your needs is not.
- Guard against cynicism and hostility.
- Sometimes it's so easy to join the cynics with "that's life." If you feel negative, stop yourself, take a few deep breaths, and change the direction of your reaction.
- If you are a workaholic, stop. Take time to find what drives the work obsession. See the sun. Smell the roses.
- Work at being an optimist. Pessimism is learned and reversible. Optimists have healthier immune systems and suffer fewer infections.
- Designate a "quiet room" in your house or apartment. This is a must with children in the house. The room should not have a TV set or a radio. It is "off-limits" while you are in it.

In our relationships with others—spouse, children, friends, coworkers—we each must establish boundaries, or "No Trespassing" signs and warnings that others will clearly understand.

- You may need to say to a spouse:
  "If you don't stop drinking and start treatment . . . "
  "I'm not going to vacuum anymore; you agreed to do it."
  "If you don't stop yelling at the kids . . . "
  "If you don't stop smoking . . . "
- You may need to say to a teenager:

"No more allowance if you drop out of school."

"No more use of our car if you quit another job."

"I think you're old enough to buy your own clothes. Let me know if you need advice."

◪ You may need to say to others:

"Quit using the name of the Lord in vain."

"I find those sexist remarks offensive."

"I'm giving up deciding what we do when we get together. You decide this time."

Such boundary setting is difficult, but it can help protect you from unwanted stress.

In addition to *psychological* boundaries, there are equally important *environmental/biochemical* boundaries that must be guarded. We cannot protect ourselves completely from these stressors, but there are actions we can take. We can't leave it to the politicians and diplomats. We can urge restrictions on companies that fill the sky with black smoke and gasoline fumes, on trucking and bus operators with diesel engines that smoke up the streets and highways, and on drivers of those gas-hungry sports utility vehicles that are so popular these days. We can support smoke-free offices, work areas, public buildings and homes. Children who live with smokers develop a high incidence of asthma, sinus problems, and upper respiratory ailments. We can support ways of turning sunlight and wind into useful forms of energy. These technologies include solar roof panels that turn sunshine into electricity and wind turbines that generate electricity.

One of the important biochemical boundaries that can easily be defended is healthy drinking water. Make sure your drinking water is purified by carbon filtration and/or reverse osmosis. Purification units are available from many sources. Do some research to find one that fits your needs. If you have well water on your property, test it frequently to make sure the quality is good.

Guarding against *iatrogenic*, or "treatment-caused," reac- tions is a boundary that is tough, but important. Many prescriptions have adverse side effects. Drugs such as diuretics, tranquilizers, calcium blockers, HRT (hormone replacement therapy), and broad-spectrum antibiotics cause problems you need to know about. Broad-spectrum antibiotics are so commonly abused that the Centers for Disease Control (CDC) and the National Institutes of Health (NIH) frequently send out warning letters about them. Two good sources for information on this subject are: *Candida-Related Complex: What Your Doctor Might Be Missing*[3] and *The Yeast Connection and the Woman*.[4]

Get involved. Ask your doctor, nurse, or pharmacist about the indications and side effects of every medication you use. Setting these environmental/biochemical boundaries helps you avoid pollution and strengthens your body's immunity and natural healing powers.

10 LIVING DEFENSIVELY IN A STRESSFUL WORLD

I'm assuming that *all* of us are smarter than any *one* of us. In other words, it is our job to share—whenever possible—what we know about how we can live defensively in our stressful and toxic world. The wisdom of families and communities has solved problems better than individual effort alone. Some scientists have call this know-how the survival of the fittest. One of the reasons I decided to write the *New Guide* was to provide you with some practical tips from our collective wisdom to use when stress grips you or your family.

You remember the many trouble arrows that can hit us, illustrated on page 13 in chapter 1. These can be divided into the six general categories shown in the diagram below.

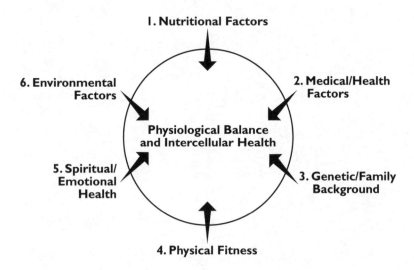

Good health is *good* balance. Illness is *bad* balance. Each of the factors shown in this diagram has the ability to upset and alter physiological balance and intracellular health. When balance is altered, you feel "sick" or "out of sorts." Your body reports imbalance with *symptoms:* headache, cough, sneezes, itches, aches, and so on. These are like the red lights on your dashboard that indicate that something is ajar or off balance.

When you experience such symptoms, you must be like a good detective or a good mechanic and try to determine what is causing the symptom. If you go to the doctor with particular complaints, a good physician should help in this detective work. If all the doctor does is treat the symptoms, then the problem hasn't been solved. It can return again—and again—to your dismay and the doctor's puzzlement.

But there are some basic guidelines that can help restore the physiological balance that signifies good health. I call them the KISS (Keep It Simple, Sehnert) Rules. They will help you and those you love live "defensively" and minimize the upsets that are so common when stress is present. So let's start at the top of the circle with nutritional factors and go clockwise from there.

KISS Rule 1: Increase Vitamin C

I learned about extra vitamin C from the writings of two-time Nobel prize winner, Linus Pauling. Although he first did research on vitamin C for the common cold and the flu, Pauling and other researchers found that it also helped against infections in general, cardiovascular diseases, arthritis, diabetes, heavy metal poisoning (lead and mercury), and a long list of other medical problems. In times of stress I recommend 1,000–3,000 mg of vitamin C per day. For the record, Pauling took up to 18,000 mg per day and lived to be ninety-three. He advocated a dose based on *bowel tolerance.* Take a larger dose every day until you get loose stools; that is Mother Nature saying, "That's enough!"

74   *KISS Rule 2: Allow for Your Health Condition*

If you have an existing medical problem or a disability following an injury or past health problem, know your limits. If you have diabetes, for example, be extra careful with your diet and medication dosage during times of stress. If you have hypertension, monitor your blood pressure more often. Whatever your vulnerability, be it a stomach ulcer or back problem or whatever, be more careful. It will pay off.

KISS Rule 3: Know Your Family

Some of us are born into families with a known genetic predisposition, such as diabetes, high blood pressure, food allergies or sensitivities, or alcoholism. Such problems can be dormant for years and not present symptoms. But in times of stress they can show up. Be aware that stress can aggravate the "glitches in your genes."

KISS Rule 4: Exercise More

During times of stress, extra exercise is essential. Sure, you might feel too tired to bother, and in times of turmoil it is very easy to interrupt one's regular walk, run, swim, or time on the Exercycle. But get back on track! Exercise is "your safest tranquilizer." It makes a difference. Do it.

KISS Rule 5: Pray More

The power of prayer in times of trouble has been tested in every religious tradition. Pray for yourself. Pray for others. Guard against cynicism and hostility. Keep in mind that it's an imperfect world filled with imperfect people. Work at being an optimist. Forgive those who trespass against you. Laugh more. Spend time with people who have a sense of humor. Give thanks for the gifts you have been given. Say your prayers before meals and at bedtime. Spend more time reading the Bible and favorite spiritual material.

KISS Rule 6: Clean the Air

Pay special attention to the quality of air in your office or work-place. People who are painters, printers, carpenters, mechanics, or lab technicians have to be extra careful about air quality. If you work in settings where chemicals, smoke fumes, or dust are present, make sure resources such as portable air cleaners/filters are available. Use special masks and clothing for protection. In normal times, the air in your environment may not get to you — but in stressful times, you may not be able to manage it. Pol-luted air can clobber you in times of stress. Clean it up.

In addition to these rules focusing on the *big* picture, here are some tips for the *small* picture. I call them stress busters:

- Stop the coffee. Caffeine is a powerful stimulant. It increases muscle tension and anxiety. Switch from coffee to green or herbal tea.
- Stretch more. By making your body more flexible, you will be more resistant to stress.
- Get some downtime. During stressful times resolve to get away for an afternoon or evening. Take a drive or a walk in the country. Listen to relaxing music. Get a relaxing massage.
- Breathe deeply. If something angers or upsets you, take four deep, slow breaths before you react. It will help keep you cool.

Remember these rules at all times, and especially when you are under stress. Be smart. Keep ahead of stress. You can do it!

Step 2
Learn How to Relax

11 MASSAGE, THE MAGIC RELAXER

Massage therapy has come a long way since my book *Stress/Unstress* was published in 1981. For example, one of my favorite magazines, *Townsend Letter for Doctors and Patients,* now has a regular monthly feature about massage and acupressure points. This column is written by Michael Blate, the executive director of the G-Jo Institute, which he cofounded in 1976. In his articles he discusses the benefits of combining acupressure and massage and tells people how to find "ouch spots," where fingertip massage triggers pain. These points can be used for relief of a wide variety of problems, such as headaches and even reactions caused by food allergies.

For further details and printed materials you may write Michael Blate at the G-Jo Institute (see Resources).

If your telephone book's Yellow Pages are like mine, you will find listings for therapeutic massage, myotherapy, and certified and licensed massage therapists. These therapists offer services such as trigger-point myotherapy and deep muscle massage. A visit to them might offer some special tips that could help you in a home program.

For centuries, people all over the world have used various types of massage to heal and relax. You can do the same. It's cheap—and it's safe. You can massage, or be massaged, by your spouse, friend, sibling, parent, or older child. The only materials needed are a lubricant such as baby oil or body lotion (special massage creams are also available), a towel, and your fingers.

Have the person you are massaging sit in a comfortable position or lie faceup on the floor. You may want to set the mood of relaxation by playing a recording of some soft, mellow music. Do the massage in a slow, deliberate manner. Encourage the person to inhale and exhale slowly and deeply during the massage, since deep breathing encourages relaxation. When you are a bit too vigorous, you will hear complaints such as "Not so hard" or "Slower, please." When you're doing it just right, you will hear the compliments "That feels good," or you may hear only a relaxed "Ahhh."

Hand Method

1. Put a small amount of oil onto your fingers. Hold one of the person's hands, palm up.
2. Stroke the palmar surface of the hand with both of your thumbs for a few moments. Then stroke the surface of each finger, starting with the little finger and ending with the thumb.
3. Rotate each finger while gently pulling it.
4. Next grasp each finger at its base, near the knuckle, and pull gently. Let your fingers gently slide down and off the fingertips. (If there is too much oil on the fingers to permit gentle pulling, wipe some off with a towel.)
5. Repeat the entire sequence with the person's other hand.

Foot Method

Before starting the massage, make sure the person's feet are clean and free of open cuts, sores, skin conditions such as athlete's foot (fungus dermatitis), or other evidence of infection. While you massage the soles of the feet, ask the person if he or she has any painful or sensitive areas.

1. Put a small amount of oil into your hands and rub it onto the first foot.
2. Hold the foot up by the ankle with one hand and rub the back of the heel with the other.
3. Use both thumbs in long, wide strokes. Stroke over the bottom of the foot. Then gently pull every toe, letting your fingers slide off the ends of the toes. Use light pressure and determine the level that feels good to the person.
4. Hold both sides of the small toe, and rotate it twice clockwise, pulling gently. Repeat this for each of the other toes.
5. Gently pinch the side of the foot and the top of each toe, starting with the small toe.
6. Using both thumbs held next to each other, press into the bottom of the foot, starting at the base of the big and second toes. Continue this down the inside of the foot to the heel.
7. Use a thumb-over-thumb technique (one thumb on top of the foot and one on the bottom) in a pinching stroke. Make pinches from the bottom of the foot up, to the end of a toe. Pinch each toe, starting with the small toe and ending with the big toe.
8. Starting at the base of the big toe, stroke across the sole of the foot with your thumb and then back across the foot just below the first stroke path. Repeat this all the way down to the end of the heel.
9. Use the tips of the fingers to apply pressure and make several circular strokes around the ankle. Then continue this circular motion over the top of the foot.
10. With your thumb, bend the big toe toward the top of the foot, and then bend it down over the sole several times. Repeat this with each toe. Be gentle, because most toes are stiff.
11. Hold the ball of the foot with the hand on that side and hold the ankle with the other hand. Guide the foot in two slow circles in each direction to rotate the ankle joint.
12. Stretch the *gastroc*, or calf muscle. With the person's leg

held straight, put one hand under the ankle and place the palm of your other hand on the upper half of the sole of the foot. Raise the leg up and hold the stretch for fifteen seconds. Be gentle. Ask the person if the stretch is long and hard enough; if not, adjust accordingly. Most people have tight gastrocs.

13. Rub the foot briskly with the towel to remove the oil.
14. Repeat the entire sequence with the other foot. Sensitive areas of feet should be worked lightly and for a longer time.

Neck Method

1. Have the person receiving the massage lie on his or her back, faceup on the floor with the head on a small pillow.
2. Kneel at the person's head. Place your knees on each side of the head and gently touch the shoulders.
3. Reach under back of head and locate reflex points (the occipital protuberance) on each side at the base of skull, shown in the drawing below. You can locate them by feeling the base of the skull behind the ear and then moving toward the spine. Follow the lower edge of the skull until you come to a slight notch or depression between the tendons of two muscles about one and a half inches from the midline. There is one of these points on each side.

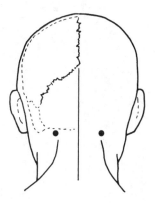

82 4. Apply firm pressure with your thumbs to each reflex point for fifteen to twenty seconds. If it is quite tender, continue applying pressure until the pain or tenderness decreases or disappears completely.

5. Now drop down along the sides of the neck for about two inches in the same trough between the muscles, and you will find the next pair of reflex points, one on each side of the neck at the level of the third cervical vertebra. Apply pressure with thumbs for fifteen to twenty seconds. Then apply a small amount of oil to the neck area and massage gently.

6. Now move to the third location, at the level of the second thoracic vertebra in the upper part of the back. The location is one inch lateral to the midline, about an inch inside of the border of the shoulder blade, as in the diagram below. With your thumbs, apply firm pressure to reflex points for fifteen to twenty seconds. It may be easier to reach this location if you remove the pillow from under the individual's head and gently support the head with your hands.

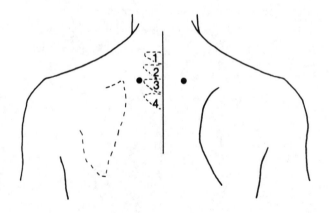

Face and Scalp Method 83

1. Have subject sit upright in a chair. You should stand behind the chair.
2. Apply a small amount of oil to the forehead and then gently massage it with your index finger, moving in circular patterns.
3. Use you index and middle fingers to gently massage around the orbital bones of the eyes in a circular motion. Continue massage of entire facial area, stroking and gently stretching the skin.
4. Next, apply the ear pull. Grasp the ear between your thumb and index finger. Gently tug down, then up, then sideways. Repeat this with the other ear.
5. Now massage the scalp, gently stretching the skin on top of the head. Cover the entire surface of the head.
6. Finally, do the head squeeze. Have the person sit straight upright in the chair, and then place the palms of your hands over both ears. Press inward against the skull as firmly as you can for fifteen to twenty seconds. Then release the pressure and repeat once more. Next, put one hand on the forehead and the other over the back of the head. Press inward with both hands and squeeze the skull as firmly as possible for fifteen to twenty seconds. Then release the pressure and repeat once more.

Neck and Back Method

1. Have the person lie facedown on a floor that is covered with carpet or a heavy blanket, with his or her head turned to the left side. Clothing may be removed from the back or left on. Kneel on the left side.
2. Starting on the upper back between shoulder blades, massage the area by making small circles with your fingertips.

84   Massage slowly upward to the base of the neck and repeat until the person is comfortable with the pressure.

3. If the back is bare, put some oil on your hands and fingers and work it in well. It will aid in the massage process.

4. Slide both hands upward on the person's left side along the entire spine to the hairline on the neck. Gently lift the head and neck up from the floor. Lower the head and turn it to the right. Repeat this on the right side of the spine.

5. Make a V with your right thumb and index finger, and then, with kneading and gently pinching actions, move your hand down the entire left side, from below the left shoulder blade down to the small of the back.

6. Now move to the other side and kneel on the right. Make a V with your left thumb and index finger and repeat the same kneading and gentle pinching actions along the right back, from the shoulder blade to the lower back.

7. With both hands, provide general vigorous massage, first to the left side of the back, then to the right. Make small circles with your fingertips. Add oil to your hands if needed.

8. Finish with gentle massage, using your fingertips to apply light strokes from the midline of the spine outward. Start at the hairline of the neck and end at the small of the back. Repeat on the other side. In order to be more comfortable, kneel to the right of the person while massaging the right side and to the left for the left side.

Which reminds me, I haven't had a back rub for quite a while, so pardon me while I enlist the help of my wife, Colleen, and see if the "first-aid kit" in her hands is still working.

12 SLEEP TIPS AND HELPERS

The headline in *USA Today* read, "The National Sleep Debt." It reported that 40 million Americans suffer from sleep disorders, such as insomnia and sleep apnea. It also reported that a recent Gallup Poll found that 49 percent of American adults—almost half—noted that they had trouble falling or staying asleep. This is an increase of 33 percent over the previous survey.[1]

Our changing lifestyles account for some of this problem. When large parts of the country were without electricity and most Americans lived on farms, people went to bed when the sun went down. Now we have cable TV and the Internet. We shop at all-night supermarkets. It's harder to get to bed at a decent hour.

Another reason is that we have longer work hours. Since 1969, each person of working age has added an average of 150 hours per year in working or commuting. The most severely sleep-deprived Americans are working moms and people who care for aging parents in addition to their regular, longer work hours.

But there is another, more significant explanation for our sleep deprivation. A study done by the National Commission on Sleep Disorders researched and identified the most common causes of sleep problems—and guess which one was first? Yes, stress was the winner.[2]

Here are the six major causes of sleeplessness:

86 1. *Stress:* Ordinary worry about stressful things at home and work is the most common cause. Stress stirs up adrenaline and increases heart rate, blood pressure, and arousal.

2. *Depression:* Studies show that 12 million Americans have depression disorders. They wake up early and have trouble going to sleep again. Sometimes the medication they take—which helps in the daytime—causes trouble at night.

3. *Irregular Schedules:* Up to 80 percent of all night-shift workers (for instance, nurses, doctors, telephone employees, twenty-four-hour grocery store employees, and security guards) have difficulty sleeping. This is because the body usually follows a twenty-four-hour sleep/wake cycle that is triggered by darkness and light. Work schedules that run opposite to the sun's rising and setting cause the hormone *melatonin* to get "out of sync" in the sleep center of the brain, so that these people are drowsy when they should be alert and awake when they should be asleep.

4. *Alcohol:* Although a recent study shows that one in six Americans uses alcohol to induce sleep, in my clinical experience, it's a bad idea. Alcohol may help you fall asleep, but it results in a light, fragmented sleep. After the sedative effect wears off in about four hours, there's a rebound effect that leaves you wide-awake in the middle of the night. This, plus having to go to the bathroom to empty your bladder once or twice, pretty well ruins the night! One drink or a glass of wine at dinner is OK, but please, no alcohol within two hours of bedtime.

5. *Caffeine:* Coffee, black tea, chocolate, cola, and many other sodas are loaded with caffeine. Caffeine's buzz lasts from six to eight hours after ingestion. If you have sleep problems, limit your caffeine intake. A cup or two at breakfast is fine, but try to avoid caffeine later in the day.

6. *Food or Exercise Too Close to Bedtime:* Vigorous exercise and eating—even a bedtime snack—can boost your body's

metabolism. This increases the heart rate, which alters sleep. The rule is: No exercise or big meals within three hours of bedtime.

What about prescription medications for sleeplessness? Several do seem to work. I have had the most success with the benzodiazepines, such as Restoril and Dalmane. Some prefer the barbiturates, such as Nembutal and Seconal. But all physicians have their favorites, and you should consult with your doctor if the nonprescription products noted below aren't helpful. (Note: The benzodiazepines and the daytime tranquilizer Valium should be used with caution by persons over sixty-five. They reduce reaction time; a recent study shows that they increase chances of car accidents by 50 percent.)[3]

I have recommended several home remedies or natural products to my patients over the years. I learned about some of their ingredients in the classic book *The Herbalist* by Clarence Meyer.[4] Many natural sleeping aids consist of combinations of the herbs listed below. Don't give up if one product doesn't work. Because some have more valerian than hops, or more chamomile extract than the others, most people have to "buy and try."

These are the key ingredients in herbal sleep remedies:

- *Valerian root.* This European plant has been used as a calmative for several hundred years. It usually comes in 100 mg capsules of standardized valerian root extract.
- *Hops.* Originally found in China and the Canary Islands, the hops plant is now grown in many forms in the United States. It is primarily used in the manufacture of beer and ale, but is increasingly popular as a sleep inducer.
- *Chamomile.* This is another old-time calmative. Many people drink chamomile tea as a bedtime beverage.
- *Melatonin.* This natural substance is increasingly popular. It was originally obtained from cacao leaves from Africa

and South America and then became a well-known remedy for preventing jet lag among the pilots of Swiss Air. Now it is widely used in northern states as a sleep aid for people with seasonal affective disorder (SAD). Many of my patients improve their sleep by starting with melatonin when the days get shorter in November and continuing it until spring.

One good source for these natural remedies is Swanson Health Products, a mail-order company in Fargo, North Dakota. One product that combines several products is Fast Asleep Night Time Herbal. It is produced by NuNaturals Inc., P.O. Box 644, Eugene, OR 97440. It is available from Swanson Health Products (see Resources).

Step 3
Nourish Your Body

13 NUTRITIONAL NUGGETS AND LIFESTYLE PEARLS

In this chapter I'll share with you some of the new knowledge that researchers have gained in recent years—the "nuggets" of information and the "pearls" of wisdom about stress. First, let's talk about nutritional nuggets pertaining to stress. In the past, stress has been considered to be strictly a psychological experience, and that is still the prevailing assumption of most doctors and patients. According to this view, stress is caused by a series of events that create the "fight or flight response" observed by Hans Selye in his work at the University of Montreal in the 1950s and 1960s. This response is "surface stuff," that is, it can be readily observed, measured, and recorded. What can't be identified so easily is the "biochemical stuff" that occurs at the cellular level, affecting organs, hormones, neurotransmitters, and all sorts of vital functions in that remarkable structure called the human body.

In addition to the stressful human events that we know about, stress also occurs following exposure to radiation (such as medical X rays), electromagnetic fields (from power lines, computer terminals, and microwave ovens), air pollution (diesel and gas fumes, chemical factories, and crop dusters), viral, bacterial, and yeast infections, medications, illicit drugs, alcohol, cigarettes, and even heavy exercise. After it takes a blow—whether psychological or electromagnetic or chemical—the body tries to right itself, to clean up, clear out, heal, and recover. It's at this point that nutritional help is vital, as so much new research is helping us to understand.

Before I get into some of this new research, I want to give
you a few nuggets.

Ten Nutritional Facts You Should Know for Sure

1. There are six basic nutrients. *Carbohydrates:* Starches, sug-
    ars, and fiber all come from vegetables, fruits, and grain
    products. Carbohydrates are a fuel, and when they are
    burned they supply the body with energy, provide bulk to
    the diet, and stimulate regular elimination from the bowel.
    Proteins: The building blocks of the body, proteins allow
    growth and repair, form hormones, build enzymes, and
    help replace injured body cells. *Fats:* They provide energy,
    form cell membranes, make hormones, and serve as carri-
    ers for fat-soluble vitamins. *Vitamins:* These vital sub-
    stances help release the energy in our food. They also help
    in nearly all chemical reactions in the body. *Minerals:* In
    addition to building strong bones and teeth, minerals, make
    hemoglobin for our red cells and provide vital links in most
    of the chemical reactions in the body. *Water:* The "forgot-
    ten nutrient," water is needed to replace fluids lost in our
    sweat and urine. It helps transport critical nutrients all over
    the body, removes wastes, and regulates body temperature.
2. Poor nutrition increases your risk for *all* health problems.
    Classic examples of serious health problems caused by
    nutritional deficiencies are scurvy (too little vitamin C),
    beriberi (too little vitamin B_3), and pellagra (too little
    niacin). But, on a smaller scale, deficiencies can also cause
    a wide variety of problems that are less threatening, but still
    significant.
3. Use sugar only in moderation. Sugars contain lots of calo-
    ries but very few nutrients. Excess sugar intake can cause
    obesity, tooth decay, hyperactive behavior in children, over-
    growth of yeast/candida infections, diabetes, and heart dis-
    ease. You can't cut down the sugar content of store-bought

candies and other goodies, but you can eat less. Try chewing more slowly to make sweets last longer. Cut down on the amounts you can control. If the recipe says one cup of sugar, try one-half cup instead, or use honey or fruit as a substitute.

4. Butter is better than margarine. Margarine is made by a process called *hydrogenation*, during which hydrogen is added to unsaturated liquids to turn them solid. This process makes this spread a troublemaker. So don't eat or use margarine.

5. Add more fish and fish oils to your diet. They contain healthy omega-3 fatty acids. Research has shown that people who eat fish regularly, such as the Inuit and the Japanese, have lower levels of heart disease. Focus on cold-water fish, such as salmon, halibut, tuna, sardines, and herring.

6. Always eat plenty of vegetables and fruit. Whenever possible, buy organic products.

7. Use salt in moderation. Try seasoning with herbs such as basil, caraway seeds, chives, oregano, thyme, and rosemary. Experiment. Be creative.

8. Keep a food journal, recording everything you eat. It's so easy to forget that donut you ate at the office. Writing things down not only helps you keep track of exactly what and how much you're eating, but also lets you see the connection between stress and eating.

9. Enlist the support of your family and friends. Eating is so often a social activity, and family members and others should be made aware of the changes you'd like to make.

10. Seek professional help if you need it. A registered dietician at your local clinic or hospital or experts at a quality weight-loss or fitness program can help you come up with an eating plan that is right for you. They can also give tips that will support your efforts.

Knowledge of some recent research on nutrition will also help you make wise choices. Here are some examples of some stress-management nutrients.

Vitamin C. Most everyone knows that there is something about this basic vitamin that supports healing in general. It shortens the common cold and helps minimize flu symptoms when taken in dosages larger than the Recommended Dietary Allowance (RDA).

C was the first vitamin to be studied. In the late 1770s, Dr. James Lind, a doctor in the British navy, found that if sailors on long cruises were given generous helpings of oranges and limes (their sailors were once called *limeys*), they did not get scurvy. This terrible disease had led to bleeding gums, blindness, open ulcers, and death for thousands of otherwise healthy young sailors, but with vitamin C it disappeared. Lind later acknowledged he had learned about this from the Dutch, who had made this discovery and always loaded up on oranges, lemons, and limes in Portugal and Spain!

Molybdenum. The function of this mineral was discovered after many patients got sick following exposure to sulfites. For many years sulfite-containing solutions were sprayed on salads at restaurants and salad bars to prevent bacterial growth, especially in warm southern states such as Arizona and California. Now such use is forbidden by state laws. Exposure to these sulfites sent many unlucky citizens to the emergency room. Some even died. Studies prompted by these emergencies found that molybdenum helps detoxify sulfites by activating a protective enzyme called *sulfite oxidase*.

Vitamin B$_5$. When heavy stress occurs, the blood flow to the gastrointestinal (GI) tract stops so that the muscles will have enough energy for the "fight or flight response." When stressful events occur repeatedly for several hours or days, the cells of the mucous membranes get low on oxygen and repair services in general slow down. The cells are "sleeping on the job" and

94   do not function normally. This disturbance in healing causes a disturbance in digestion and absorption, which can lead to bloating, arthritic pains, headaches, fatigue, and an imbalance in the brain chemistry that causes "brain fog."

Also called pantothenic acid, vitamin B_5 plays a key role in helping the GI tract to recover. It works along with the amino acid called L-glutamine and vitamins A, C, and E to rebuild the *mucosa*, or inner lining, of the digestive system.

Vitamin B_1. Shortages of this vitamin, also called thiamine, causes beriberi, which was first observed in Malaysia, southeast Asia, and the Philippine Islands. People afflicted with beriberi are too sick to do anything, even walk or talk; indeed, *beriberi* means "I cannot" in the Sinhalese language. It was found to be prevented by eating brown rice (hulls and all) instead of purified, cleansed white rice.

An interesting historical note: During the Japanese conquest of Malaysia and Singapore, the "brown soldiers" (from India, Pakistan, and Egypt) were fed brown rice while in prison camps and did not get beriberi and other ills. The "white soldiers" (from England, Canada, and Australia) ate white rice and got a wide variety of ills, including depression and even schizophrenia!

Niacin. Another B-complex vitamin, niacin was found to prevent pellagra. Once very common in the southern United States and the Caribbean, pellagra makes the skin very pale. Exposure to the sun makes the skin of people with the disease thick and rough. The patient also gets indigestion, diarrhea, and then severe constipation. If not treated, patients can become insane. Dr. Joseph Goldberger (1874–1925) of the U.S. Public Health Service proved the disease was the result of dietary deficiency of niacin and other B-complex vitamins.

It was from the early studies of such deficiency diseases that the RDAs (Recommended Dietary Allowances) were established for vitamins A, B_6, and C and minerals such as magnesium, calcium, and iron. For instance, the RDA for vitamin C is 60 mg, for B$_6$ is 1.8 to 2.2 mcg. However, the dosages now recommended by nutrition experts such as Dr. Jeffrey Bland and the dosages I recommend in my clinical practice are much greater. I myself have taken 2,000 mg of vitamin C per day for several years and have never had a cold in all that time. As for vitamin B$_6$, Kilmer S. McCully, M.D., a respected researcher at the Veterans Affairs Medical Center in Providence, Rhode Island, and an expert on the prevention of heart and vascular disease, recommends as much as 10 to 25 mcg for persons with family histories of early onset arteriosclerosis. That has also been my recommendation, with 4.0 to 4.3 mcg for younger patients and those with fewer heart problems in the family.[1]

Prior to the discoveries of Lind, Goldberger, and others, food was considered to be merely a source of energy for our body. Now we know it has many, many more functions. In addition to those we've just examined, vitamin D prevents rickets, and vitamin E helps extend the life span of red blood cells and acts as a powerful antioxidant (as do vitamins A and C). Now a whole new area of research is looking at phytonutrients, or phytochemicals from plant foods. Many have complicated names such as lignins, polyphenols, glucosinolates, cyanidins. They puzzle biochemists and physicians alike, but in his excellent new book, *The 20-Day Rejuvenation Diet Program*, Dr. Bland carefully and accurately defines them.[2] In times of stress, these nutrients are especially helpful not only in prevention of trouble but in the recovery process.

Carotenes are phytonutrients found in the orange-red families of fruits and vegetables. Carrots are a classic source. Carotenes are close relatives of the *bioflavonoids* and the *anthocyanidins*, pigments from grapes, cranberries, and pine bark that form *pyknogenol*. Carotenes can be quickly converted to vitamin A. Vitamins A, C, and E are all antioxidants and defend the body against smoke, smog, foreign chemicals, and other

96   forms of stress. *Selenium, zinc, copper, and magnesium* are trace
       minerals that also help in the antioxidant process that is needed
       in times of stress.

When one gets into discussions about "antioxidants" and
"excessive oxygen" and "biological rancidification," many
patients and doctors run for cover—as do many biochemists.
However, the explanation given by Dr. Bland is one of the best
I've heard, so I'll let him give the details.

> We live in a world of apparent contradictions and para-
> doxes, and these contradictions extend to oxygen. We
> need oxygen to live, and fortunately, it is plentiful, mak-
> ing up 20 percent of the air we breathe. The body uses
> oxygen in metabolism, the process which enables it to
> convert protein, carbohydrate, and fat from foods into
> energy for cellular repair, immune functions, muscle
> contraction, nervous system function, reproduction,
> digestion, and a myriad of other activities.
>
> Beneficial though oxygen is, it is not without haz-
> ard. Oxygen has a dark side. It is a reactive chemical
> substance and in certain forms it can be harmful to the
> body. In much the same way as the combination with
> iron produces rust and eventually brings about the
> breakdown of products made of iron, oxygen in certain
> forms combines with the biological building materials
> of the body and causes them to break down. Although
> our bodies don't rust, they do undergo a process called
> biological rancidification, in which oxygen causes dam-
> age by combining with fats (lipids). . . . The way bio-
> logical rancidification occurs in the body is similar to
> how oxygen combines with fat in a cube of butter and
> causes it to become rancid.[3]

Research done by C. D. Davis, Ph.D., and J. L. Greger
has shown that other trace minerals such as manganese, copper, zinc, and selenium help form detoxifying enzymes in the

liver to get rid of stressful toxins in our food. They combine to make a detoxifying enzyme in the liver called superoxide dismutase, or SOD.[4]

Some physicians, such as Victor Herbert and John Renner, say that vitamin supplements such as those noted here are excessive, arguing that if you just eat a well-balanced diet you get all the vitamins and minerals you need. I wish it were that simple, but it isn't. I side with Dr. Jeffrey Bland in recommending supplements. You can get all the beta carotene you need by eating two or three raw carrots each day, but to get 400 mg of vitamin E, you would have to eat fifteen cups of fortified cereal or thirty-two ounces of sunflower seeds. For the recommended 1,000 mg of vitamin C, you would have to drink five cups of fresh orange juice. Copper and selenium are found in root vegetables, whole grains, and liver, but, unfortunately, it is hard to get enough of these minerals in our regular diet. So many of us, caught up in the hurry, hurry of everyday living, far too often fail to eat and drink in ways that are best for our health — especially in times of stress. Therefore, I recommend Dr. Bland's "Insurance Formula," illustrated in the table below.

Rejuvenation Program "Insurance Formula" for Daily Nutritional Supplements[5]

Nutrient	Dosage Range
Vitamin B_1	5–10 mg
Vitamin B_2	5–15 mg
Vitamin B_3 (niacinamide)	20–50 mg
Vitamin B_6	10–20 mg
Vitamin B_{12}	20–100 mg
Pantothenate	20–100 mg
Folate	400–800 mcg
Inositol	30–50 mg
Natural vitamin E mixture	50–300 mg (60–400 IU)

Natural carotene mixture	5–20 mg
	(5,000–15,000 IU)
Vitamin C	200–1,000 mg
Vitamin A	2,500–5,000 IU
Vitamin D	50–400 IU
Bioflavonoid complex	20–100 mg
Biotin	50–300 mcg
Calcium (citrate or hydroxyapatite)	100–400 mg
Magnesium (citrate or glycinate)	100–200 mg
Iron (chelated)	5–15 mg
Zinc (chelated)	10–20 mg
Manganese (chelated)	5–10 mg
Copper (chelated)	1–3 mg
Chromium (nicotinate)	50–200 mcg
Selenium (complex)	50–200 mcg
Iodine	50–100 mcg
Molybdenum	50–100 mcg

If you are one of today's "walking wounded" because of stressful events, you need more than three balanced meals. Learn the "Ten Nutritional Facts You Should Know for Sure" (pp. 91–92). Blend them into your eating habits and recipes. Become a lifelong learner about nutrition so that you can undo stress-caused damage and build up your reserve power.

14 MAINTAINING YOUR PROPER WEIGHT

Former U.S. Surgeon General C. Everett Koop officially declared war on obesity and all the health problems associated with being overweight. The problem is, he didn't say much about how to maintain proper weight. Although I was never a general, I was a lieutenant commander, and even though I can't declare war, I can run up a battle flag. With it I can give you all some practical advice that I have followed personally and shared with my patients over the years.

The average citizen these days is inundated with information about how to fight the flab. Are they paying attention or merely being confused? I think we can simplify it. Recently I helped Tamorah Mahnerd write a workbook for weight management, *Keys to A New Life: Psychological and Biochemical Insights about Weight Loss.*[1] In it we outlined many useful methods for achieving proper weight, not just for severely overweight people, but for ordinary people like John in chapter 1.

Let's start with the obvious. There is no doubt that many Americans move too little and eat too much. We spend an average of two hours each day driving to and from work and doing errands in our cars—that is all sitting time. When we get to work, many of us are sedentary—at the desk, at the computer, at meetings. When we end our day at home in front of the TV, we sit for another couple of hours. Children and teens average more than three hours in front of the tube each day. The result of all this sitting around is that about 50 percent of Americans are overweight.[2]

100   Over recent years I have worked with many patients who
have weight problems. I have pulled together some things I
have learned with them into what I call the "Ten Commandments for Proper Weight."

1. *Exercise more.* Set aside a regular time each day for fifteen
   to twenty minutes of exercise. Whether it is running, jogging, walking, biking (indoor or outdoor), swimming,
   weight training, or whatever, do it four or five times a week.
   Whatever you do should make you puff and sweat a bit.
   (My own exercise is jogging and stretching exercises. People in our neighborhood can set their watches at 8 A.M.
   when I run by.) Add to your exercise routine "friendly
   detours," simple actions that get you to move rather than
   staying put. Try using the stairs instead of the elevator or
   escalator. When you drive to shop or go to work, park at the
   far end of the lot and walk to the door. When you drive to
   church, don't park next to the church but in the neighborhood a block away and walk to the church. When you need
   to mail a letter, walk to the mailbox. This kind of incidental
   walking, plus that everyday work at home raking leaves,
   mowing lawns, shoveling sidewalks, ironing, housecleari-
   ing, and gardening, will burn up 150–200 calories per day.

2. *Limit the number of meals you eat away from home.* Eating out
   can be hazardous, because helpings are too large and usually contain more than a thousand calories each. My advice
   is, when you do eat out with someone, do what my wife,
   Colleen, and I do — split the meal. We order one serving
   and ask the server to bring two plates. If you are alone, eat
   half a serving, ask for a "doggie bag," and take the other half
   home for another meal. Careful ordering also helps; order
   things like a grilled chicken sandwich, chicken salad with
   low-cal dressing, a vegetarian dish, or, for simplicity's sake,
   a baked potato with a low-fat topping.

3. *Minimize social events that are "eating events."* Many social
   events arranged by friends and family go all out with lots of

the best food. Such events often lead to overeating. Minimizing these occasions will take some engineering, but it will help reduce your anxiety, lower your stress, and ensure successful weight management. Suggest another activity that doesn't involve food or make your apologies: "I'm sorry, I have a conflict" is the truth if social eating is a problem! I don't expect you to become a hermit, but try to be selective for a month or two if you are trying to lose weight.

4. *Use veggies and fruits for snacks.* When you just "gotta have" a snack, get out the carrot sticks or celery, slice a banana, pear, or apple (you know the adage). I also recommend dried apricots, dried prunes, and a new favorite of mine, dried cranberries (or *craisins*). All are healthy and helpful snacks.

5. *Go "nuts" with nuts.* There is a common misconception that nuts are bad because they contain fat, but they are really good foods. They contain vegetable fat, which is good for you, and more important, they contain proteins that help you control spells of hypoglycemia (low blood sugar). I frequently mix chopped nuts with my breakfast cereal or oatmeal. Raw nuts are the best option, but the more common roasted varieties are fine.

6. *Eat at regular times.* Being regular helps set those important biorhythms our body prefers. Try three meals a day on a schedule you can usually keep. Avoid long periods without eating, which can lead you to lose control and binge on high-calorie foods or candy. Instead, plan a regular schedule and stick to it.

7. *Drink more water.* Make it a rule to have two glasses of water (preferably filtered, distilled, or even the sparkling kind) with each of your big meals. A six-ounce glass of juice with breakfast counts as one serving of water. Then have a glass of water at midmorning, another glass of juice with lunch, and more water at midafternoon. Water is "body-friendly" in many ways. It takes up space in your stomach, helping

you feel full without calories. It also helps in the digestive process and in better absorption of the food you eat.

8. *Eat and chew slowly.* This is easier said than done. As members of a rush-rush society, we have learned to eat fast. We gulp down those calories without thinking. Usually people who eat too fast eat too much. Taste the food. Enjoy it. Mix talk and laughter into your meals. Chew slowly and you'll get fewer calories because you will feel full before you overeat. It works.

9. *Eat less.* As we get older, we need less food. Our metabolism slows down from the high pitch of our adolescent growth and activity. Take smaller portions. Try two pieces of pizza instead of four. Eat half a sandwich instead of a whole.

10. *Think before you drink.* By that I don't mean just alcoholic beverages, but all soft drinks, even the diet variety. Another contemporary temptation is the stylish coffeehouses at every major intersection in every town and city. They provide you with trendy beverages such as cappuccino and caffè latte that are loaded with steamed milk and whipped cream. It is easy to pick up 150 to 200 calories per drink. A word to the wise: Think before you drink.

These Ten Commandments apply to children as well as adults. Studies have shown that an overweight child is not as likely to be picked for the team and will find it harder to make friends. Overweight teens are more likely to be shut out socially than those with a handicap or physical challenge of some kind. Yet research shows that more and more children in America have trouble maintaining proper weight. A recent report in the *Journal of the American Society of Bariatric Physicians*, stated, "At least one in five kids today is overweight, a 50% jump in the last two decades."[3] With these numbers, everything said in this chapter regarding maintaining proper weight also pertains to the younger set.

Should you follow these Ten Commandments? Are you ready to push the panic button or start making New Year's resolutions? When are you overweight?

The best guide I've found is the BMI or Body Mass Index, described in chapter 5. If you are of average build, here is a simple way to calculate your BMI: Multiply your weight (in pounds) by 703. Then divide by your height in inches, squared. The result is your BMI. The number should be less than 27.

Here are some examples:
Jane's weight is 140 lbs. Her height is 5 ft. 5 in. (65 inches).
$$140 \times 703 = 98,420$$
$$65 \times 65 = 4,225$$
98,420 divided by 4,225 = BMI of 23 (normal)

Dick's weight is 210 lbs. His height is 6 ft. (72 inches).
$$210 \times 703 = 147,630$$
$$72 \times 72 = 5,184$$
147,630 divided by 5,184 = BMI of 28.4 (high)

The dividing line between normal and high BMI is 27, according to the experts I've talked to. Dick's score of 28.4 puts him into the 33 percent of Americans who are considered overweight. If Dick follows my Ten Commandments, he can pull that BMI down under 27. I know he can do it, and so can you.

Step 4
Exercise Away Stress

15 | EXERCISE, YOUR SAFEST TRANQUILIZER

Exercise, exercise, exercise. Every magazine you pick up, every newspaper you read has articles on exercise and ads for exercise equipment—treadmills, cross trainers, workout attire, and sport shoes. There's an article on women's kickboxing (a hybrid of karate and boxing) as a great way to work off weight and get a whole body workout while working out aggressions in a safe environment.[1] There are articles on the value of walking and how many corporations such as L. L. Bean and Monsanto Chemical, and school districts such as Westside Community Schools in Omaha, Nebraska, provide fitness centers where their employees receive credits and money to attend classes that encourage exercise.[2]

Yes, exercise is an essential part of our world, partly because of its many health benefits, including:

- ☒ Improved cardiovascular efficiency;
- ☒ Reduction in LDL (low-density lipoproteins);
- ☒ Increase in HDL (high-density lipoproteins);
- ☒ Maintenance of proper body weight;
- ☒ Better attention to health habits in general;
- ☒ Improved stress management.

I want to discuss that last item, "improved stress management." What is it about exercise that makes it a useful tool for managing stress? Why is a dose of running or brisk walking usually better (and safer) than a dose of tranquilizers? One of the first documented studies about the mental health value of exercise was done at the University of Wisconsin in the 1970s. John Greist, a psychiatrist, did a study that showed that jogging was better than psychotherapy as a treatment for depression. In a pilot study, eight clinically depressed patients participated in a ten-week running program. The patients walked and ran, both alone and in groups, from two to seven times a week. Patients were interviewed every two weeks by computer, ensuring that the data about their health was collected without the intervention of a possibly biased human interviewer. Six of them were cured of their depression. Most recovered from their depression after the first three weeks of the program and maintained their recovery with regular exercise. Greist noted that this cure rate of 75 percent was substantially better than the recovery rate for similar patients treated with the traditional psychotherapy he and his staff offered. He and his team of psychiatrists and psychologists expanded the study to another twenty-eight depressed patients. They found that for most, thirty to forty-five minutes of jogging three times a week was at least as effective as talk therapy.[3]

Dr. Ronald M. Lawrence, founder and president of the American Medical Jogger's Association, an organization with more than three thousand members, observed, "Man was meant to be a moving animal, but he's become sedentary. Distance running can bring us back to the basics of what we're here for." Although there is no hard evidence yet, some researchers believe that running cures mental problems by changing chemicals in the body. A Purdue University professor of physical education, A. H. Ismail, reported "significant relationships" between changes in hormone levels of joggers and improvements in emotional stability. Skeptics of his study say that the out-of-shape professors he studied at Purdue felt better simply because they got away from their desks. Ismail still sticks to his theory that exercise produces chemical changes.[4] One lay observer, Clinton Cox of the *New York Daily Times*, adds his two cents to the debate over such cures: "It's almost impossible

108   to worry about your job or other such mundane pursuits when your body is in total agony!"[5]

Whatever the researchers claim and the skeptics seek to disprove, several things are apparent. Vigorous exercise is helpful for many, including myself. It blows out mental cobwebs and calms everyday tension. For some it is probably as effective as tranquilizers and alcohol—without the dangers, risks, and side effects. As Colman McCarthy of the *Washington Post* put it, "Raising one's pulse focuses the mind more clearly than raising one's glass." McCarthy suggested that the Senate Finance Committee consider giving tax deductions to those who use their lunch hour for a two-mile run instead of a two-martini stupor. McCarthy noted, "Two miles through the park clears the head, restores a sense of identity, relaxes the blood vessels and sends a person back to the office ready to conquer the world—or at least that part of it resting in the in-basket!"[6]

Probably 5–10 percent of the population can't do vigorous exercise because of cardiovascular problems, marked obesity, musculoskeletal disease, and circulation problems involving the spine and lower extremities, but even these individuals are helped by walking, stretching, and gentle exercise. The biggest problem is that 150 million men and women get little or no exercise. They are the "sedentary citizens" who never walk when they can ride, use elevators and escalators whenever they can, and have no regular exercise routine. At night they are the couch potatoes with a TV remote clutched in their hand as they surf the channels. Exercise would help them—and you—get off the couch, lose weight, smoke less, sleep better, feel better, and manage stress better.

So here is your exercise plan:

Step 1. Make Up Your Mind and Gear Up Your Body

One of the easiest ways to gear up is to work exercise into your daily routine. Here are some tips to start:

- ☒ In the morning, get up a half hour early and take a brisk walk, jog, or bike for fifteen minutes before breakfast.
- ☒ When you take public transportation, get off the bus or the train several blocks early and walk the rest of the way.
- ☒ At noon, instead of going to the cafeteria or restaurant for lunch, brown-bag it and exercise for a half hour with the time you've saved.
- ☒ After work, instead of two martinis or two beers before dinner, try two laps around the block.
- ☒ If you're bored at home or have time on your hands, sweep the sidewalk or shovel the snow in front of your house or apartment.
- ☒ When you go on an outing to a museum, art gallery, the beach, or visiting, make exercise as essential part of the outing. Try some skipping, tag, Frisbee throwing, volleyball, or whatever is fun to do with family or friends.
- ☒ Do your yard or home chores at a faster rate than normal. As you make the bed, vacuum, sweep, mow, rake, chop wood, shovel snow, speed it up a bit!
- ☒ Turn regular walking into exercise—lift your heels off the floor and add an extra spring to your step. While strolling, tense your calf muscles or stretch the hamstrings in your upper legs.

Step 2. Choose Your Thing

There are different strokes for different folks. Look at this list or make up your own and choose something you enjoy doing:

archery	fencing	jogging
badminton	football	judo
baseball	golf	jumping rope
basketball	handball	karate
bicycling	hiking	Ping-Pong
bowling	horseback riding	racquetball
canoeing	horseshoe pitching	rowing

110

running	soccer	walking
sailing	squash	water-skiing
skating	swimming	wrestling
skiing	tennis	

Whatever you choose, find something you *like* to do. In developing an exercise plan it's essential that you understand this maxim: "Go for satisfaction, not for accomplishment. Do whatever you need to do to make exercise fun." What's fun to do is good for you.

Step 3. Start Your Plan

Here are some tips from fitness experts to consider while you are developing your plan. They apply mainly to running, but are equally applicable to all vigorous exercise programs.

- *The talk test.* You should be able to talk while you exercise. If you can't, you're working too hard or going too fast, and should slow down.
- *Warm up and cool down.* Always do stretching and warm-up exercises before starting and after completing your exercise. Do leg and back stretches, push-ups, and sit-ups.
- *Don't be intimidated.* Don't let faster runners, better tennis players, or more experienced bikers intimidate you. Do your own thing at your own speed in your own way.
- *Learn your body's capabilities.* If you are uncoordinated, some competitive sports or activities may be frustrating. If you are tight-jointed and stiff, you may need calisthenics for several weeks before trying some sports or activities.
- *Learn to take your resting pulse.* Because your pulse is needed as a guide to aerobic activity, you should learn to take your pulse at your wrist: With your hand held palm upward, place the index and middle fingers of your other hand on the inside of your wrist near the base of your thumb. Then, with the aid of a watch that measures seconds, count

your pulse for thirty seconds and multiply by two. The normal resting pulse for adults is sixty to seventy beats per minute, about one second per beat. For children it will be slightly faster.

◩ *Learn your target pulse.* In the early stages of training check your heart rate to make sure you aren't exercising too vigorously. To calculate your target pulse, subtract your age from 220, then multiply by 85% (.85) if you are fit or 70% (.70) if you are not in top shape.

Step 4. Work at It

After you have geared up, chosen an exercise, and developed your skills, remember that any good exercise should involve these six elements:

1. *Movement.* Vigorous movement such as walking, biking, hiking, or jogging burns up calories. It has been said of many overweight Americans that it's not that they eat too much, it's that they move too little.

2. *Stretching and deep breathing.* Because deep breathing and stretching are known to help relieve tension and help us relax, they should be part of the exercise you choose. Inhale with deep breaths to fill up your lungs and force all the air out when you exhale. Agility and flexibility, or the range of movements in the joints, are as important as muscular endurance and strength. Spinal flexibility is especially important. So bend, twist, and swing.

3. *Vigorousness and promotion of aerobic activity.* Any exercise you choose should be intense enough to increase your heart rate and make you perspire. It should be sustained for fifteen to twenty minutes to provide the training effect called "aerobic activity." The frequency should be at least three times a week.

4. *Enjoyment.* If an exercise program is to be successful, it must be done regularly. To be done regularly, it must be

112   enjoyable. When it's enjoyable, it's relaxing and gives physical, mental, and social benefits. Have fun when you do it.

5. *Appropriate pace.* It may take three or four months of regular training to achieve your target pulse. Don't be in a hurry. On your "slow days," you may not feel like doing as much, but that's OK. On "fast days" when you feel great, however, be careful that you don't overdo.

6. *Good equipment.* An essential part of any exercise is quality equipment and comfortable shoes. The ritual of putting on your exercise togs helps set your mental attitude and prepare your body for the exercise.

I want you to know that I practice what I preach. I've been a jogger and biker for more than twenty-five years. In ten years I haven't missed a day of work because of colds or flu. Patients and people say, "Doc, I hope I look as good as you when I get to be your age!" The human body is the only machine I know of that breaks down when you don't use it. Exercise is not only the safest tranquilizer, but also an excellent "wellness pill." Try it.

16 UNSTRESS EXERCISES

Breathing deeply and stretching to relax is instinctive to all of us. We've all felt tired, tense, and irritable. We've all needed to unwind, to relax. We instinctively yawn and stretch our arms and bodies. Then we can begin to relax and unwind. Deep breathing and stretching are Mother Nature's way to help us relax (which helps us be less tense) and to unwind (which means to loosen up).

But there is also another bonus—more energy! Researchers still don't know why, but enhancing spinal column flexibility increases the functions of both the endocrine and the cardiovascular systems. You feel better in general. Chiropractic and physical therapy experts tell me that the deep breathing and spinal flexion exercises described below, which I call the "Magic Seven," stretch and strengthen a group of muscles along the spinal column and between the ribs called the *intercostals*. When exercised, they get stronger and help maintain healthy vertebral alignment. This, in turn, improves the capacity and efficiency of the lungs and the cardiovascular system in general. When the intercostals work better, you feel better. Following the Magic Seven helps various nerve centers and glands that lie along the spinal column and increases your energy levels. The cumulative effect is that you "recharge your batteries."

Probably the most experienced person regarding these changes is my longtime friend Ron Fronk, Ph.D., founder and president of Turning Point Resources in Phoenix, Arizona. With his Master Motions Self-Study videotapes and seminars

114   he has trained more than four hundred clients to use his programs (see Resources). They in turn have written him with
scores of testimonials:

> I've been a medical doctor in family practice for over
> twenty-one years and was very skeptical. After three
> weeks, however, I noticed a very real positive change in
> my energy level and stamina. . . . I'm encouraging my
> patients to use it.

> I'm fifty years old and have had chronic back problems
> since my teen years. Since starting the program, other
> than a little aggravation in the beginning, my back has
> been pain free. I cannot remember when it's been better.

> It seemed like I was tired all the time. I've been prac-
> ticing [the exercises] religiously for about nine weeks.
> My energy level has shot up to where I rarely feel tired
> and I'm actually getting less sleep than I used to. I
> know it's the program because I'm not doing anything
> else different.

> In addition to being a licensed hypnotist, I've attended
> numerous personal and business seminars over the past
> twenty to twenty-five years. . . . Recently I've gone
> through some pretty traumatic times, personally and
> professionally. I was amazed at how well I managed my
> thoughts, my perceptions of what was happening, and
> my emotions.[1]

I use these exercises myself at least three times a week. After
you have read my instructions and tried them a few times you
might want to order Dr. Fronk's instructional tapes. They are
helpful, especially the Coaching Tape.

In addition to the benefits of stress management and
increased energy, there are some other practical, everyday

issues. The Magic Seven are *convenient*—they can be done most anywhere, at home, in the office, or on trips, and twenty to thirty minutes of practice can fit into most busy schedules; *compact*—no special equipment or clothing change is needed; and *cheap*—you don't have to join a sports club, take special classes, or schedule counseling sessions.

Research is beginning to find explanations for why these breathing and stretching exercises help people look and feel better. Some are rather complex. However, to follow the KISS Rule, I will explain what I have learned, after long discussions with various experts, in simpler terms.

Victor Youcha, a chiropractor and Board Certified Acupuncturist from Saint Louis Park, Minnesota, explained it well.[2] He first approached it from the energy level, pointing out that when people are stressed their entire body is uptight. That means that nearly all the muscles in the arms, legs, neck, and so on are in "fight or flight mode." It takes a lot of energy to stay in this combative mood. Blood is shunted away from the digestive tract, the lungs, and the internal organs. Normal healing and repair work get put on the back burner. Stretching and deep breathing start the reversal of this process, so the body can unwind and normal healing processes take over again.

These exercises take discipline, but they are worth the effort. When we are too inactive and sedentary trouble begins. For example, the intercostal muscles of the ribs shrink up, ligaments shorten, and the vertebral bones get fewer calcium deposits. In addition, the electrical and neurochemical functions that regulate your brain, spinal cord, and adrenal and endocrine functions get sluggish, and you have less energy.[3]

The old axiom, "Use it or lose it," is at work here. J. H. Wedge, M.D., professor and head of orthopedic surgery at the University of Saskatchewan, describes this in *The Natural History of Spinal Degeneration*.[4] His research shows how lateral nerve entrapments, subluxation, and disc degeneration occur from slouching, sitting, inadequate exercise, and so on—especially when you

116   add that nasty stress. This is why the Magic Seven will be helpful to you. But, like learning to play golf or tennis or the piano, you need to practice—and practice. You didn't get in trouble overnight, and you won't get back to normal overnight—but you will make progress.

Here are some tips for using the Magic Seven that I have found useful:

▧ Select three or four of the exercises and do them in a quiet place. Do them slowly five times. As you improve, increase the number to twenty-one times. Eventually, after a month or so, try adding another two or three exercises until you can do all of the Magic Seven.

▧ Don't be surprised if you have some sore abdominal and back muscles at first. If you get leg cramps, stand up and stretch your legs. If your back gets stiff, ease up for a few days.

▧ If you experience a little "acid stomach" (which occurs when bending causes a reflux of stomach acids into the esophagus), try a few antacid tablets.

▧ Some of the exercises may make you dizzy. I find it helps to keep my eyes open.

▧ Find the time that is best for you. I do my Magic Seven in the early evening, at about eight o'clock. Find a comfortable spot on a rug or carpet. Make it a pleasant experience.

▧ Do what you can comfortably do. If you have some back or other problems, you might want to consult a physician, chiropractor, physical therapist, or other health professional before you start.

Here are the Magic Seven Unstress Exercises:

I. Ground Up

1. Take your shoes off and stand upright with your feet shoulder width apart, toes pointed slightly inward, with the head, neck, and spinal column comfortably erect.
2. With your hands together, dominant hand inside passive hand, raise your hands and arms high above your head. Gently stretch up and arch slightly backward.
3. Exhale completely, through your mouth, as you simultaneously swing your hands and arms down between your legs and bend your knees as if you are going to sit on a chair.
4. Slowly begin taking a deep breath, through your nose, and slowly begin straightening your knees and trunk as you raise up your body. As you do this, push down on your legs and insides of feet as if you're trying to spread apart the ground between them.
5. With your body comfortably erect again, stretch your hands as high above your head as you can and arch back slightly as you complete the deep breath.
6. Repeat steps 1 through 3 up to twenty times, for a total of twenty-one.

Caution: On occasion people lose their balance when they close their eyes. Therefore, because you're standing, *always* keep your eyes open.

II. Spin Up

1. With your eyes open, stand erect with your feet six to twelve inches apart and knees slightly bent.
2. Stretch your arms and hands, palms down, straight out from the sides of your body like wings at shoulder height horizontal to the floor.
3. Turn or spin around slowly to the right like a helicopter.
4. Repeat steps 1 through 3 up to twenty times, for a total of twenty-one.

Note: In the beginning you may be able to do only two or three rotations. That's fine! Stop and sit or lie down until you get your balance back, and then repeat the process. Slowly but surely, you'll get up to the goal of twenty-one spin-ups without stopping.

Caution: Because of the potential dizziness, *always* keep your eyes open, and *always* practice in a safe, open area so, if you happen to fall, you won't hurt yourself. In the beginning, most adults are able to spin around only a few times before getting dizzy. When you feel even *slightly* dizzy, even if it's only after one turn, stop and sit or lie down until the dizziness disappears. To help reduce dizziness, do what dancers and figure skaters do: Pick out some object that you can focus on, and keep your eyes on it as long as you can while turning around. In other words, as you turn to the right, focus your eyes on the object until you can no longer see it over your left shoulder, and then quickly turn your head around to the right to see the object over your right shoulder again.

III. Legs Up

1. Lie flat on your back on the floor, with your face up.
2. Extend your arms along your sides, palms down.
3. Point your fingers slightly inward to the center of your knees.
4. Close your eyes to make the exercise more reflective.
5. Raise your head and tuck your chin into your chest.
6. Inhale slowly and deeply, through your nose, as you raise your legs straight up from the floor.
7. Exhale slowly and completely, through the mouth, as you simultaneously lower your head and legs to the floor.
8. Repeat up to twenty more times, for a total of twenty-one.

Note: Keep your knees as straight as possible throughout the exercise. In the beginning, some people have difficulty doing this. If so, bend the knees as needed to finish the complete motion. Rest assured, however, that you'll improve until you're able to completely raise and lower your legs with ease and keep your knees perfectly straight throughout.

Note: Deep breathing is vital and highly beneficial; as best you can, completely empty and completely fill your lungs with each repetition.

IV. Head Up

1. Kneel with your head, neck, and spinal column comfortably erect.
2. Place your hands on your lower buttocks.
3. Close your eyes to make the exercise more reflective.
4. Exhale completely, through your mouth, as you lower your chin to your chest.
5. Gently stretch your head and neck back over your shoulders as far as you comfortably can. Inhale deeply and completely, through your nose.
6. Continue the stretch by arching backward, bracing yourself with your hands and arms on your lower buttocks, as far as you can comfortably go while completing your deep breath. The goal is to extend back until your head is above your heels.
7. Return to the starting position.
8. Repeat up to twenty times, for a total of twenty-one.

Note: Deep breathing is vital and highly beneficial, so, as best you can, completely empty and completely fill your lungs with each repetition.

V. Trunk Up

1. Sit on the floor with your legs straight out in front of you about hip width apart.
2. Hold your head, neck, and spinal column comfortably erect.
3. Extend your arms behind you slightly, placing your hands on the floor with your palms facing down and fingers pointing forward.
4. Close your eyes to make the exercise more reflective.
5. Exhale completely, through your mouth, as you lower your chin to your chest.
6. Gently stretch your head and neck back over your shoulders as far as you comfortably can.
7. Lock your arms in place at the elbows and begin taking a deep breath, through your nose, as you raise your pelvis and entire trunk up as high as you can. (Note: Now your entire trunk is parallel to the floor, held up on one end by your arms and the other end by your legs from the knees down.)
8. Tense every muscle in your body.
9. Exhale slowly through your mouth, relax, and return to the starting position.
10. Repeat up to twenty more times, for a total of twenty-one. Periodically during your repetitions of this exercise, kneel or stand in a comfortably erect position, let your hands and arms hang loosely beside you, and shake them several times to release the tension and balance the energy.

Note: Please remember, your goal is to do each exercise twenty-one times. However, few people can do this in the beginning. Do what you can, and work toward increasing your repetitions each week. Even if you do only three repetitions the first week, if you increase the repetitions by two to three each week, it will only take you seven to ten weeks to get to twenty-one.

VI. *Butt Up*

1. Kneel down with your knees, lower legs, and hands on the floor. Feet should be pointing backward and fingers pointing forward.
2. Keep your head up and your arms and legs straight as you gently permit your back and hips to drop down toward the floor.
3. Close your eyes to make the exercise more reflective.
4. Tuck your chin to your chest. (Note: Your arms and legs remain straight throughout this exercise. Your back, however, will be arched up from your hips to your neck.)
5. Inhale slowly through your nose as you raise your butt as high as comfortably possible. Your arms and back, your legs, and the floor should form a triangle.
6. Tense all your muscles for two to three seconds.
7. Slowly lower your pelvis as low as is comfortably possible for you without touching the floor.
8. Exhale completely through your mouth as you gently stretch your head and chin up and back as far as they will comfortably go.
9. Tense all your muscles for two to three seconds.
10. Repeat up to twenty more times, for a total of twenty-one. When you have completed your repetitions, kneel or stand in a comfortable position. Let your hands and arms hang loosely beside you and shake them several times to release tension.

VII. Back Up

1. Kneel down with your knees, lower legs, and hands on the floor. Feet should be pointing backward and fingers pointing forward. Head should be up and facing forward. Back should bend naturally toward the floor.
2. Close your eyes to make the exercise more reflective.
3. Gently stretch your head and chin to your chest and simultaneously move your hips forward. Your back will automatically arch upward like a cat's.
4. Inhale deeply and completely through your nose as you bend backward onto your lower legs. Your trunk will remain horizontal to the floor as you continue descending until your forearms are touching the floor. (Note: Your head remains tucked to your chest, your hips remain forward, and your back remains arched until you rise up to return to the starting position.)
5. Slowly rise up to the starting position. Simultaneously exhale through your mouth, relax your back, and raise your head up as high as it will comfortably go.
6. Repeat up to twenty more times, for a total of twenty-one.

124　*Back Stretch*

1.　Now that you've finished the Magic Seven, you have one final assignment. Stretch out on the floor on a rug or blanket. Do some quiet breathing.
2.　This restful period is also a good time for prayer and meditation.
3.　After a few minutes you may feel—or even hear—a click or two as one or two vertebrae slide back into place. It is not unlike the click you may hear during chiropractic or osteopathic adjustment or physical therapy work.
4.　Your session is over. Congratulations! Repeat the Magic Seven two or three times every week.

Step 5
Care for Your Spirit

17 THE ABCs OF YOUR EMOTIONS

Our sprits are closely related to our emotions, which can be explained in both psychological and the biochemical terms. Both are complex, but understanding them will give you better control during times of stress.

Psychological ABCs

The psychological explanation for emotions was originally developed by Maxie C. Maultsby at the University of Kentucky and continues to be one of my favorites. He used a simple analogy of a horse and its rider. In this model, the thinking part of the brain—the rider—receives information from the sense organs, the eyes, ears, nose, taste buds, and skin. The limbic or feeling part of the brain that controls gut feelings—the horse—goes wherever the rider directs it. In other words, like a rider who directs a horse with reins, voice, knees, and heels, the Thinking Brain directs the Feeling Brain with the thoughts that arise from sensory experience.[1]

Your Emotional ABCs   127

The Reins	A.	*Sensing Brain:* Your perceptions, or what you see, hear, touch, and taste.	Sense Organs
The Rider	B.	*Thinking Brain:* Your evaluative thoughts—positive, negative, or neutral thinking about your perceptions.	Neocortex
The Horse	C.	*Feeling Brain:* Your gut or emotional feelings—positive, negative, or neutral—that are triggered and maintained by your thoughts.	Limbic System

Our perception of any event will determine our emotional response. The sensation of raindrops on your forehead might bring a negative emotion if you are a tennis player just beginning a long-scheduled match with your friend. But, if you are a drought-stricken farmer, it might evoke a positive, joyful emotion: "Thank God for the rain!" Or, if you are a secretary on the way to her office, the raindrops are neither "good news" nor "bad news" but merely a slight inconvenience, so the emotional response is neutral. Thus emotional habits—like all habits— have been learned, and they can be unlearned. The same can be said of beliefs and attitudes.

Habit

☒ In our model of emotional ABCs, a habit is an A-C or A-B mental process. Certain sensory perceptions evoke the same emotions every time, without going through the Thinking Brain. Or certain sensory perceptions evoke the same thoughts every time, without necessarily moving to emotion.

128   ☒   Emotional habits—like physical habits—must be learned and can be unlearned.

  ☒   Habit learning requires time and diligent practice.

  ☒   Habit unlearning requires *more* time and *more* diligent practice.

Belief

  ☒   A belief is an *articulated form* of habit.

  ☒   Beliefs are A-B mental connections made habitual by repeated movement between A, perceptions, and B, thought.

  ☒   Persons are always aware of their beliefs because they have to *think* them through before they *speak* or *write* about them.

Attitude

  ☒   Attitudes are *unarticulated beliefs*, mental connections made habitual by repeated movement between A, perceptions, straight to C, emotion.

  ☒   People are often unaware of their attitudes because they *don't have to think* them through.

  ☒   Most people explain attitudes as *spontaneous reactions*, such as, "It made me feel good."

This helps explain why most people can change bad habits, such as drinking, smoking, or overeating. They can also alter or dramatically change beliefs and attitudes. Yet what about those of us who try and try to change bad habits, to lose weight, or to stop abusing alcohol, but can't ever get the job done? They experience the yo-yo diet, regaining the forty pounds they've just lost, or they start smoking or drinking again after doing "all the right things" to quit. What's wrong with them? Is it just weak will-power or is something else out of kilter? Often it remains a mystery to them, their families, and even their doctors. Yet much has been learned in the past fifteen years about bio-chemical and nutritional factors in habitual behavior.

Biochemical ABCs

Biochemists, neurophysiologists, and nutritional researchers have learned that the chemistry of our brains includes hor-mones and neurotransmitters, including opioids, GABA, sero-tonin, dopamine, and norepinephrine. These biochemicals induce or inhibit every single impulse or thought that comes from our brains.

A stressful event can set off a chain reaction in the brain's chemistry. First, any type of stress causes opioid levels to dimin-ish. Low opioid levels automatically cause an increase in dopamine release and lower GABA levels. This in turn causes an increase in norepinephrine release. This process creates a sense of urgency, discourages slow, deliberate, and logical thinking, and can also cause a person to become irritable and easily angered. Finally, low GABA levels also cause a decrease in serotonin levels, which makes sleep difficult and produces irritability and cravings for food and alcohol. Many people find relief from these feelings from an artificial opioid that is released by alcohol and other drugs.

The synthesis of serotonin, a hormone we are learning a lot about these days, is heavily dependent on the availability of L-tryptophan and other important amino acids, including DL-phenylalanine, L-glutamine, valine, leucine, and isoleucine. L-tryptophan is especially important because it is a key building block for serotonin.

Being from Minnesota, the Land of Ten Thousand Lakes, I use the analogy of a new lake called *Lake Serotonin*. No, don't call the Minnesota Department of Natural Resources or the American Automobile Association to ask where that lake is, because it's right in your head. When the waters of Lake

Serotonin are low, your canoe hits rocks and can even run aground. When your serotonin level gets too low, you hit "rocks" and experience emotional "bumps" with symptoms including depression, poor sleep, irritability, brain fog, poor memory, unexplained cravings for sweets, alcohol, and perhaps drugs such as cocaine or heroin, in the case of addiction.

Many of our popular antidepressants, such as Prozac, Zoloft, and Paxil, belong to a class of prescription drugs called *selective serotonin re-uptake inhibitors* (SSRIs). They alter the serotonin levels in the brain by modifying its function with decreases in serotonin turnover. This leaves more serotonin to do its work.

Norman Sussman, M.D., of New York University School of Medicine and director of psychopharmacology research at Bellevue Hospital Center in New York City, has done extensive research not only on SSRIs but on the nutritional basis and formation of serotonin.[2] In recent years he has been researching potential ways to increase the availability of brain serotonin through nutritional intervention. One of these is through increasing the amount of L-tryptophan in our diet.

Until several years ago, L-tryptophan was available in tablet form and widely used as a home remedy for sleeping problems, an early sign of lowered serotonin levels. However, a contaminated lot of L-tryptophan from Japan caused an outbreak of eosinomyalgia syndrome, which involves elevated eosinophil counts, walking impairment, severe muscle aches, and shortness of breath. It even led to some deaths. The FDA banned the compound for several years, and it is now available by prescription only.

There are dietary sources of fundamental tryptophan. Spirulina seaweed capsules contain about 500 mg of this amino acid. Other natural sources include roast beef (250–500 mg per 3.5 ounce serving), roasted chicken (338 mg per 3.5 ounce serving), salmon (242 mg per 3 ounce serving), cottage cheese (312 mg per one cup serving).

Another supplement that I find helpful and use myself is called Restores. It helps me sleep better, and when I feel a midafternoon or early evening low blood-sugar level, I take two or three capsules (see Resources). So, when stress is at a high level, increase your intake of these items.

Other respected researchers have written about serotonin and its role in good mental health, including Dr. J. Wurtman and Drs. L. N. Yatham and M. Steiner.[3] By educating yourself about both the psychological and the biochemical influences on your emotions, you can go a long way toward managing your stress.

18 SPIRITUAL GROWTH THROUGH PRAYER

Since *Stress/Unstress* was published in 1981, many in the medical community have changed their attitudes about faith and prayer in the healing process. In the 1980s, if you had asked the average doctor, "Can prayer, faith, and spirituality really improve your physical health?" you might have heard, "Well, maybe, but there are no scientific studies to prove it." In the past, no self-respecting M.D. would have dared to propose double-blind controlled studies of something as intangible as prayer. The reason was that for most of the past century western medicine has been trying to rid itself of "mysticism," and that included prayer and meditation.

But things have changed. As Jeffrey Levin of Eastern Virginia Medical School in Norfolk has said, "People, a growing number of them, want to examine the connection between healing and spirituality."[1] Now a growing body of scientific evidence shows that spirituality *can* improve your health and wellness. Studies at leading medical centers on both coasts, led by Dr. Herbert Benson of the Mind/Body Medical Institute at Boston's Deaconess Hospital and Harvard Medical School and Dr. Elizabeth Targ, a psychosocial oncology researcher at California Pacific Medical Center in San Francisco, have shown that prayer and church attendance do make a difference.

Other helpful studies are being carried out at Dartmouth Hitchcock Medical Center in New Hampshire and the University of Rochester in New York. David Felton, chairman of the University of Rochester's Department of Neurobiology, has observed, "Anything involved with meditation controlling the state of mind that alters hormone activity has the potential to have an impact on the immune system."[2] Other medical schools are also embarking on research and education on the subject. The Center for Spirituality and Healing at the University of Minnesota has developed an extensive program for medical student involvement under the guidance of Dr. William Manahan.

I have also emphasized prayer with patients in my practice. My own personal experiences have strengthened my belief that God has made us stewards not only of the money we make and the land and air we use but also of ourselves—our bodies, minds, and spirits. I also believe that laypeople can and should be involved in their spirituality as well as their health care. Such new roles require increased personal responsibility and action. Little will happen if people maintain the traditional passive, dependent roles and assume that someone out there—the doctor, the pharmacist, the nurse, the priest, the minister—has the responsibility for their spiritual and physical health.

Taking our spiritual and physical stewardship seriously makes more sense if we try to understand the incarnation, broadly speaking, as God's continuing presence among us. Many people hold to the concept that God is a remote being somewhere "out there" in the distant cosmos. My own conviction has always been that God is present through the Holy Spirit in all creation. I see God in the birth of a baby, the hands of a surgeon, the laboratory of a scientist, the earth of the farmer's field, the skill of an artist, the music of a composer, the souls of ordinary people. I have felt the Holy Spirit at work in myself and in my family. This has been experienced in many small ways over the years and once in a most dramatic way.

This was in the misfortune of one of my daughters, Cynthia, who shortly after her birth developed a serious infection. This led to her becoming profoundly deaf in the first month of her life. At first my wife and I responded, "Why

134   Cindy?" "Why us?" These are the anguished questions raised by all parents who learn that their child is deaf, blind, disabled, critically ill, or injured. It is the question asked by parents who learn of their child's death in a car accident or military encounter.

Initially, Colleen and I felt feelings of hopelessness and helplessness. We prayed fervently that Cindy would "hear and speak." We felt anger and guilt. We wanted prompt, definitive action from God. When it didn't come over the next year or so, we felt disillusioned.

Then one night, many months and many prayers later, it happened. I had been in Chicago on a business trip and was returning home on the train. It was a bitterly cold winter night. I was in my sleeper car when the train stopped so suddenly at a siding that I was awakened. I pushed up the window shade to see where we were. As I looked out on the snow-covered countryside, I saw a full moon shining behind the crossbars of the railroad crossing. Something forced me to fix my eyes on the sign. Soon the crossing sign became a giant crucifix. I was transfixed by what I saw—and heard. From out of the cross came a brilliant light and a remarkably calm voice that said, "Don't despair. Out of the misfortune of your daughter will come benefits for many." Then the voice and the cross disappeared, and I was left with an experience that changed my attitude about many things.

I am still overcome with emotion when I think of it now, more than thirty-five years later. What did it mean for me? For my wife? For our daughter?

For Cindy it meant that she eventually did "hear and speak," although with a 95-decibel hearing loss she must "hear" through her skilled lipreading. She can "speak" with sign language and a remarkably good voice, considering she has never been able to hear her own voice. Cindy did well in high school, where she was a varsity swimmer. Later she qualified for the U.S. team that went to the World Games for the Deaf in Bucharest, Romania. She graduated from college and is now a staff member of the U.S. Environmental Protection Agency in Kansas City. There, in addition to other duties, she specializes in environmental education for children. Cindy is married and has two daughters.

For Colleen and me, Cindy's deafness meant that we worked to help her get the best education at home and school. It meant thousands of hours helping other parents, individuals, and children through the Alexander Graham Bell Association for the Deaf and Sertoma International's Hearing and Speech programs. Our efforts, with God's help, have brought benefits to many, estimated at one time in the tens of thousands. We helped ourselves and our daughter by helping others.

It also started me on the long-term program that I now describe as Productive Prayer, a kind of meditation. It helped me learn to feel the presence of the Holy Spirit. It taught me the meaning of Christ's prayer in the Garden of Gethsemane, ". . . yet not what I want but what you want" (Matt. 26:39).

I see a solid medical rationale for helping people gain a healthier spirit. It helps the whole person improve. In helping people develop plans to lose weight, stop smoking, start jogging, I find that many are disappointed to find out that willpower alone is often not enough. Old negative habits can often be changed only with the addition of new positive habits or as a result of changes from the new habits. For example, one over-weight man I worked with had been a heavy cigarette smoker for twenty years. He had vowed many times to quit, but he had always failed in the past. But this time he succeeded, because he also took up cross-country skiing. He found it was difficult to smoke while skiing and also a bother to carry cigarettes. He stopped smoking, lost weight from the exercise, and feels better about himself—all at the same time.

Changing emotional habits also requires taking on new, more positive habits. Promises to be kinder or be more under-standing often don't work alone. Attempts to change behavior are more successful when you feel better about yourself or

136   when you have a more positive relationship with the Holy Spirit. This allows Christ's words and attitudes to become a part of your makeup so that you gain the qualities of kindness and understanding you seek. This benefits your physical health as well. When you feel better about yourself, your relations with others, and your Christian priorities in life, your chances of achieving a healthier body and mind greatly increase. It makes medical good sense to have spiritual growth.

How does one exercise for spiritual growth? A whole panorama of religious activities exercises the soul: reading the Bible and other devotional materials, listening to religious music, viewing art with religious themes, doing acts of charity and goodwill, participating in formal and informal worship, participating in various church activities, praying and meditating. Like individual fibers in a tapestry, each act of worship, prayer, meditation, and fellowship contributes to the fabric of spiritual life.

Productive Prayer

Productive Prayer is a method that has helped me to exercise my spirit. I use it to supplement my traditional habits of worship and prayer. Use it, and I predict it will lead to spiritual growth for you.

1. *Find a quiet time and place.* There should be no phones, radios, or television, and no interruptions. I do the Magic Seven exercises and pray in our bedroom in the hour before bedtime. In this frenetic world of ours, the early morning or late-night hours are often the only time to avoid interruptions.

2. *Get ready.* To prepare my body and relax my muscles, I do some stretching and slow, deep breathing. Controlled breathing is an important part of preparation. I inhale through my nose and exhale through my mouth, with my exhalations twice as long as my inhalations. This kind of breathing has a tranquilizing effect.

3. *Take a relaxed position.* I assume a kneeling position, bowing at the waist to put my forehead on the floor. By this time my body is relaxed and my mind is clear. If I am still tired or tense about some personal problem, I may do a few more exercises.

4. *Pray.* I start by repeating three or four times the phrase, "Dear Father in heaven . . . " I pray about personal or family problems or concerns: "How will I keep my Christian priorities?" "Which way will I turn?" "What is the answer to the problem?" "What can I do to help?" I may offer prayers of intercession, thanks, or celebration during the five- to ten-minute interval that follows. I often feel the presence of the Holy Spirit during the prayers.

5. *Finish the exercises.* I conclude with another period of stretching and slow, deep breathing. The total time from beginning to end is twenty to twenty-five minutes.

6. *Read the Bible and other devotional materials.* When I get up from the floor, I spend five or ten minutes in this kind of reading. Shortly thereafter, I retire for a good night's sleep.

You Can Be Changed

One summer my family and I attended worship with a small congregation in the Bemidji–Cass Lake area in northern Minnesota. The sermon that Sunday, a dialogue between the pastor and one of the elders, was entitled "If God Could Speak." The pastor read the part of a man who was saying the Lord's Prayer, and the church elder, a retired college teacher with a beautiful, deep voice, read the part of God.

As the Lord's Prayer was recited, the voice of God interrupted to ask questions: "How closely do you follow these requests?" "What do the words and phrases mean?" This dramatic method challenged the man who had been automatically rattling off the words, and forced him to rethink their true meaning. It reminded me of what C. S. Lewis said in *The Screwtape Letters:* "Simply to say prayers is not to pray."

138   The sermon brought home to the man, and to the congregation, the value of prayer. The voice of God concluded by saying, "Prayer is a dangerous thing. You could wind up changed, you know!" That, of course, is the point of spiritual growth. You could wind up changed—changed in your perceptions, changed in your Christian perspectives, changed in the way you deal with others. You could wind up changed in the way you handle stress.

19 SPIRITUAL GROWTH THROUGH STRESSFUL TIMES

Can one grow spiritually in times of stress? As we say in Minnesota, "You betcha!"

After a terrible car accident, after the death of a spouse or child, or after a natural disaster such as a flood or a tornado, people ask those difficult questions: "Why do bad things happen to good people?" "Why me?" "Why us?" In more than forty years as a family doctor, I've been asked these "why" questions many times. The best answer I've been able to give is: "We don't know why, but we can learn from it."

But it's tough to convince the parents of the college student who was killed in a snowmobile accident, or the citizens of Jarnell, Texas, who lost twelve children and teenagers in a tornado, or the people of Grand Forks, North Dakota, who lost their homes, businesses, and farms in the Red River flood of 1997, or the one thousand former employees of that successful company that went belly-up. The skeptics can say with some credibility, "Wait a minute. People don't learn from tragedies, they just suffer! Severe stress just plain destroys people!"

Can we learn from stress? Can we become wiser? Well, the family and friends of the college student encouraged the legislature to pass a law requiring crash helmets, driver's education, and licensing for snowmobiles in Minnesota. The citizens of Jarnell will pay more attention to tornado sirens and have emergency training in schools next year. The Grand Forks area will see lots of watershed engineering, dike construction, and movement of homes to higher, safer sites.

OK, so people learn and make changes as a result of *major stress*, such as that just described, but what about less severe stress? Here are some examples I've seen firsthand in my patients (the names are changed but the cases are real).

Lisa, a thirty-two-year-old single woman, is an accountant who recently was dismissed from her company after eight years of loyal work. The explanation she received was downsizing, but she knew it was more than that. She had been at odds with her supervisor for several years. Then she had a major conflict with him over some of her accounting procedures. Her bitter reaction to the layoff caused her a lot of stress: "It made me mad. I'll never forgive him. Sometimes I lost sleep over it. Sometimes I got a headache." Later on she and several other staffers who had also lost their jobs formed a support group at Lisa's church. "One of the things I learned was to forgive him." Her motto became, "Forgive and forget." Lisa now has another job with the accounting department of a Fortune 500 company. "I feel fine and like both my job and my new supervisor. I'll always remember what our group leader at church said, 'Forgiveness is granted believers as a free gift.' I learned a lot!"

John, a forty-three-year-old married man, worked as a carpenter. He was doing some repair work on a roof when he slipped on the ladder, fell off, and broke his ankle. He applied under workers' compensation for several weeks of coverage while his ankle healed. During the round of meetings, doctors' offices, and comp claims offices, he met many other workers who had been injured on the job—and had experienced all the miseries that followed. When he observed how many had violated safety rules, he decided to go to a night and weekend college program to become a certified safety engineer. "I learned from my accident and decided to help others. I like my work. Maybe my guardian angel gave me a shove off that ladder. I've thanked him many times!"

Speaking of guardian angels, our own family encountered such an angel many years ago. Our entire family—Colleen,

Kristie (age nine at the time), Cindy (age six), Sarah (age three), and I—was vacationing in Colorado. We were hiking up a steep trail alongside a mountain stream, which a heavy rain earlier that morning had filled with roaring water. As we got to a bend in the trail and a sunny spot in which to rest, the three girls ran ahead and prepared to take off their shoes to soak their hot feet in the cool water of the stream.

My ever-vigilant wife, seeing one of the girls stand up on a nearby rock, shouted, "Don't stand on that rock, you might slip and fall into the water!" Kristie and Sarah heard the warning but, because of her deafness, Cindy couldn't hear the warning. She stood up on the rock—and in a flash slipped and fell into the fast-moving stream.

Colleen and I were on our way to join the girls when the accident occurred, and for a moment we were both stunned. Then I threw off my backpack and jumped into the stream. I grabbed Cindy with one arm as she was swept near me. I tried to stand up but the rocks were slippery, and we both went tumbling down the fast moving stream. We were swept under water several times.

Within a few minutes I was exhausted by the intense struggle to swim ashore with Cindy in my arms, and we both sank under water for what seemed an eternity. I thought to myself "We're going to drown!" During that terrifying moment, Colleen saw what was happening and prayed in a loud voice, "Lord, please help them. Please send help, Lord!"

By that time we were fifty yards downstream from her. Then I caught sight of a tall man alongside the stream with his arm outstretched to help us. Holding Cindy in one arm, I stretched out the other to him, and he pulled us up on the bank.

Our rescuer was very tall. He had the longest arms I'd ever seen, and I jokingly said, "You must be a basketball player. You saved our lives!" He didn't reply for a while but smiled warmly and looked at me with eyes that had a mysterious blue quality. Then he said, "I was glad to be here to help."

With that he disappeared. By then Colleen came running down to where Cindy and I collapsed on the ground. Breathlessly Colleen asked, "What happened? How did you get out? Are you both all right?"

"Yes," I gasped and handed Cindy to her, "that man pulled us out."

Colleen was amazed. "What man? I don't see anybody." I looked around. He was gone—nowhere to be seen!

What happened to us that day? I couldn't explain anything except we had been saved from drowning! Long afterwards, Cindy said, "That man who saved us was our guardian angel, wasn't he?"

Colleen's prayer for help was answered. Prayer saved Cindy's life, and it saved my life. The accident and our rescue helped our family understand the power of prayer. It's a classic example of learning—profound learning—from stress.

Recently, Kristie sent me a clipping from the *San Diego Tribune* that got me thinking about how tragedy and stress can change things. The headline read: "Sex Offender Committed in Girl's Killing." This was a story about the nationwide passage of Megan's Law, which requires that communities be informed when convicted sex offenders are released in their area. It was of special interest to Kristie and her husband, Karl, because the tragic original kidnapping and horrific slaying of seven-year-old Megan Kanka had taken place in what was then their neighborhood.

The Sunday after reading that news release, my wife and I were at our home church, where we sang one of my favorite hymns, "This Is My Father's World." As I puzzled over horrible events like Megan's death, we sang this verse:

> This is my Father's world
> Oh, let me not forget
> That though the wrong seems oft so strong,
> God is the ruler yet.[1]

"Though the *wrong* seems oft so *strong . . .*" Out of Megan's 143
senseless killing has come a law that may save many little girls
and boys from death and abuse. Out of misery can come
change. Out of misery can come words of comfort from friends
and neighbors. Out of misery hopefully can come forgiveness
and sympathy. Out of war and conflict can come peace.

Saint Francis of Assisi said it this way:

Lord, make me an instrument of Your peace,
Where there is hatred, let me sow love;
Where there is injury, pardon;
Where there is doubt, faith;
Where there is despair, hope;
Where there is darkness, light;
And where there is sadness, joy.

O, Divine Master, grant that I may not so much seek
To be consoled as to console,
To be understood as to understand;
To be loved as to love.

For it is in giving that we receive;
It is in pardoning that we are pardoned;
And it is in dying that we are born to eternal life.

Over the years I have developed what I call the Special Seven
Stress Helpers. They can be used with prayer and meditation to
help in relationships especially in times of stress.

1. *Accentuate the positive.* Take time each day to think posi-
   tively about yourself and muse about the good things in
   your life. Give thanks for the gifts you have been given. Say
   a prayer before each meal and at bedtime.
2. *Eliminate the negative.* Spend less time with hostile, negative people who add little to your emotional well-being and
   subtract much. In times of trouble seek the solace of prayer
   and meditation.

144   3. *Fill your cup of goodwill.* Spend more time with gentle, pos-
       itive people who add much to your emotional well-being
       and subtract little. Plan an outing with your spouse or mate
       at least once a week—a movie, a hike, a concert.

   4. *Do what you enjoy.* Budget some time each week for fun
      things such as sports or hobbies—any activity that offers a
      change of pace. Join the choir, coach your child's softball
      team.

   5. *Remember that it's OK to have a few warts.* Accept your own
      flaws and those of others as part of life. Ask for forgiveness if
      you step over the line. Don't let the three Ps—Power, Pres-
      tige, and Prosperity—become too important to you.

   6. *Collect people, not things.* Try to maintain a well-rounded
      life that offers growth for mind, body, and spirit. Remember
      the three Ss—Share, Serve, and Submit.

   7. *Grant yourself wisdom and courage.* Enjoy the rich heritage
      of your faith tradition and let more of its music and litera-
      ture stir your soul and nourish your spirit. Understand and
      observe the sanctity of religious, family, and cultural tradi-
      tions such as Good Friday, Easter, Rosh Hashanah, Thanks-
      giving, Christmas, Yom Kippur, the Fourth of July,
      birthdays, and anniversaries.

   "Why do bad things happen to good people?" The answer is
a mystery, but crises can help us grow spiritually, change our
perceptions, and change the way we deal with others. They can
change us for the better. Thanks be to God.

20 DEVELOPING YOUR PERSONAL ACTION PLAN

The brochure for the seminar on stress management says it will help participants learn "how to stay calm and productive under pressure." They will learn behavior modification skills that can give them "greater ownership of their lives" and help them avoid emotional "self-sabotage." Throughout the well-designed brochure are clever cartoons of people who obviously are sabotaging themselves because they can't stay calm and productive under pressure.

This seminar's goals are much the same as the goals I've developed in my many seminars on stress management. They are the goals I hope you will embrace in reading this book. When stress hits you or your family, practice what you've learned so far. Reach for these goals:

- Avoid overreacting emotionally and hurting your relationships both at home and at work.
- Avoid and change habits of procrastination, disorganization, and conflict that can be related to stress.
- Be calm and clearheaded in situations when you might have lost your temper before.
- Avoid overeating and say "no" to too much food, even when you crave it.
- Stay productive and positive when you feel overwhelmed.

But remember, stress has a way of sneaking up on you. As the old Spanish proverb says: "It is not the same to talk of bulls as to be in the bullring." As Tim O'Brien states so well in his

146   news article on stress, "Stress management works well when we have a definite plan and apply it daily. However, there are times when we get into unexpected situations. Or, we face situations that are more intense than we thought they would be."[1]

O'Brien's article offers five suggestions for dealing with these situations:

1. Have a specific stress management and relaxation training program. Practice your techniques every day. Allow relaxation to become a natural habit.

2. List the events or situations that have caused you excess stress in the past. Honestly assess how you have performed under pressure in the past. What were your biggest challenges? Where and when did you perform well? Knowing your strengths and working to remove your weaknesses begins with honest self-appraisal.

3. Have confidence that you can handle whatever comes along. Realize that everything probably won't go perfectly. However, if you've set up and practiced stress management techniques regularly, they won't let you down under pressure if you remember to use them correctly.

4. If you lose your temper or become upset, focus on your breathing to regain control. Remember, your breath follows your awareness. And your awareness follows your breath. If you're angry, breathe deeply with your diaphragm. If you become depressed, try to breathe more with your chest and faster than normal. Don't hyperventilate, just breathe a few extra times each minute. Also, try to remove yourself from the situation for a minute or two while you regain your composure.

5. Keep reminding yourself, "This, too, shall pass." If a situation feels unbearable or unending, try to think of when it will be over. Focus on a positive time after the present challenge passes. The sun will rise tomorrow. The seasons will change on schedule. Life does go on.

In addition to O'Brien's five suggestions, I would add two more tips:

6. In times of stress express gratitude to others for help and advice, even if you feel too grumpy to do it. Thank them for their kind act. You might be pleasantly surprised to learn that your gratitude has opened the door to more help just around the corner. In any case, it will make you feel better.

7. Prepare yourself now for times of unusual pressure by practicing your stress management techniques today. Then, when you really need them, they will be there to help you through the tough times, too.

In addition to these very important and helpful insights about handling ourselves in stressful times, there is an equally important goal for us as Christians. What Paul says in 1 Corinthians 3:16 opens up another crucial door about ourselves and others: "Do you not know that you are God's temple and that God's spirit dwells within you?"

If you take Paul's words literally—and I think everyone should—then you must look upon your body as a "holy place" or "God's temple." It is a building that must be kept "shiny clean." Learning to better manage stress is just part of keeping the temple clean, because, as we've seen, many researchers have shown that psychological stress alters the body's chemistry and impairs its healing ability. In times of stress it is especially important to practice good nutrition, get regular exercise, avoid junk and fatty foods, minimize the use of nicotine, alcohol, and caffeine, and prevent damage to your temple.

Roland Seboldt, who was book editor at Augsburg Publishing House when I wrote *Stress/Unstress*, wrote some special words of wisdom about self-care:

Care of the body is caring for the Spirit's temple and is an act of worship . . . We must also take care of our soul (spirit) and mind. It is so easy to pollute them. In a television study by researcher Vicki Alt she found that talk shows blur boundaries of right and wrong. There are no boundaries in today's culture. Nothing is forbidden. Television emphasizes the deviant (so often) that it becomes the normal. Caring for God's temple means that as we avoid media pollution in the laudable way, we are also learning to avoid pollution of our air, soil and water![2]

With that sort of challenge, it's time to start the planning process. You are now ready to develop your Personal Action Plan. But first you need to have some background information. Experts in psychology and sociology have discovered that there are six major sectors that can be indentified in the life of each of us: spiritual, family, financial/business/professional, physical, social, and mental. One way to visualize this is the concept of the Wheel of Life shown below.

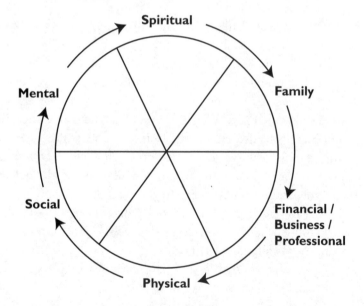

The priorities assigned to each sector vary from person to person. We all know people who devote a disproportionate amount of time to one sector at the expense of others: executives who spend nearly all their time and energy on company business (financial/business/professional) or people who pursue, on a nearly full-time basis, club or community activities (social). Such one-sided individuals choose a certain sector and follow it with such intensity that children, spouse, physical health, spiritual life, and other aspects can be left by the wayside. This can lead to a variety of problems.

Preliminary Planning

First let's assume there are some things you'd like to change. Briefly answer the following questions:

- What pleases you most about your life so far?
- What has been your most important accomplishment so far?
- If you had your life to do over again, what would you want to do differently?
- What do you *expect* to do with the rest of your life?
- What would you *like* to do with the rest of your life (if different from the preceding question)?
- What is your purpose in life? Being considered successful by others? Accumulating money? Achieving fame? Raising a healthy and happy family? Being a good member of your church/synagogue?

Next, on a sheet of paper list everything you can think of that makes you feel good. Write down as many things as possible in one sitting, and then give yourself a few days to add others to the list as you think of them. For example:

- Listening to George Gershwin music
- Taking a walk with my dog
- Camping with my kids

150
- Hiking in the outdoors with my spouse
- Going to church/synagogue with my spouse/family/friends

Then, on another sheet of paper make a wish list, a list of things you would like to gain, possess, or accomplish in your life. For example:

- I wish there was something I could do for my spiritual life. I'd like to go on a retreat to think about things for a week.
- Our kids are growing up so fast. I would like to take them to Disneyland in the next year or so.
- I'd like to lose thirty pounds in the next six months.
- I want to be more creative.
- I'd better think of changing jobs.
- I wish I could become a good cross-country skier. I think the exercise would help me.
- I'd like to finish my college degree before my daughter graduates from high school.
- I wish we could get a bigger house so the children could have their own bedrooms; then perhaps there wouldn't be so much arguing at home.
- I'd like to get a part-time job so I can learn some business skills.

Setting Goals

Now, take six pieces of paper, one for each sector in the Wheel of Life. On the top of each sheet write one of these sectors: Spiritual; Family; Financial/Business/Professional; Physical; Social; Mental. Look at your "wish list" and put each item on your list into one of the six sectors. If there are some sectors you aren't certain about, leave them blank for now. Put your wishes in the middle of each page.

For example:

1. *Spiritual*
   Go to a church retreat.

2. *Family*
   A bigger house.
3. *Financial/Business/Professional*
   Get a part-time job.
4. *Physical*
   Lose thirty pounds in the next six months.
5. *Social*
   Join the choir or couples club at church.
6. *Mental*
   Finish my college degree.

Next, across the top of each of the six pages draw a horizontal line and add numbers from 0 to 10. Then, in the most honest and objective way you can, mark with an "X" the number on each line indicating where you are today in that sector, in general. Then pick the number that indicates where you would like to be on the scale in one year, if you had your way. Place an X with a circle around it there. Make sure these goals are your goals and not the goals of someone else, such as parents, teacher, spouse, or friend!

Now, on the bottom left-hand side of each page list the probable benefits you could receive if you achieve the wish or goal you set for that sector. For example:

- Make spouse feel happy.
- Enjoy my kids more.
- Make me feel better.
- Give me more freedom.
- Help me avoid illness or premature death.
- Have money to go on a trip to Disneyland.
- Bring me closer to God.

Share your goals and benefits with someone you trust, someone who will react to them in a positive, helpful way. Think about it for a few days and make sure you are comfortable with what you have written down on the bottom left side of the page.

152   With the help of this same person, try to identify barriers or boundaries that might obstruct the pathway toward the goals you have set. List them on the bottom right. For example:

- ☒ I'm too busy with my five kids to take a class.
- ☒ Even with my overtime work at the plant, mortgage money is so expensive!
- ☒ My dad would never let me do it.

Finally, think of ways to get around the barriers.

Personal Wellness Contract

To commit yourself to following through on your Personal Action Plan, you may want to use the following Personal Wellness Contract.

I, _____, having completed my Personal Action Plan, agree to use this contract to improve my fitness level, control stress, and improve my general health status for the interval from:

Start date: _____

Finish date: _____

I realize that change is difficult, especially when changing long-established emotional habits regarding eating, exercising, and lifestyle. I also realize that practice and diligence will be required to polish the new skills I will learn. However, I now agree that I am ready to begin such change, and my signature on this contract is evidence of my commitment. Now with my concerted effort, plus the help of God, my family, friends, and associates, I pledge to follow the attached Personal Action Plan.

Signature _____

Date _____

The Personal Wellness Contract you have signed is more than an attention grabber. It indicates more than that you have finished this book and agree to control stress more effectively—and creatively—and that you plan to follow through with a plan based on some well-thought-out goals. It testifies a commitment to rethink your responsibility for the body, mind, and spirit that has been entrusted to you by God.

NOTES

Chapter 1
1. Hans Selye, *The Stress of Life* (New York: McGraw-Hill, 1978) p. 62.
2. Jeffrey Bland, *The 20-Day Rejuvenation Diet Program* (New Canaan, Conn.: Keats Publishing, 1997).

Chapter 2
1. Milton Friedman, *Money Mischief* (New York: Harcourt Brace Jovanovich, 1992).
2. Erling Podoll, letter to author, September 1997.
3. Peter Tompkins and Christopher Bird, *The Secret Life of Plants* (New York: Harper and Row, 1997).
4. Theresa Podoll, letter to author, October 1997.
5. Karen Youso, Jim Buchta, and Donna Halvorson, "New Houses in Minnesota at Risk for Moisture and Rot" and "Owners of Ailing New Homes Find Few Places to Turn for Help," "Asthma and Lingering Illnesses Lurk in Tainted Air of Flawed House," *Star Tribune* (Minneapolis), October 12, 15, 18, 1997.
6. C. Ford Runge, "Tackle Global Warning Sensibly," *Star Tribune* (Minneapolis), October 18, 1997.
7. M. D. Lemouick, "Courting Disaster," *Time*, November 3, 1997, p. 65.

Chapter 3
1. C. Noel Bairey Merz, "Heart Disease: The Stress Connection," *Time*, May 10, 1997.
2. Mary Lamielle, "Accommodating MCS Sufferers," *Indoor Air Review*, March 1995, p. B1.
3. Quoted in W. Lambert, "More Claim Chemicals Made Them Ill," *Wall Street Journal*, January 17, 1995, p. B1.
4. Robert Haley, "Gulf War Syndrome," *Journal of the American Medical Association*, Jan. 15, 1997, Vol. 277, p. 231-7.
5. James Braly, *Dr. Braly's Food Allergy and Nutrition Revolution* (New Canaan, Conn.: Keats Publishing, 1992).
6. Christine Winderlin and Keith W. Sehnert, *Candida-Related Complex: What Your Doctor Might Be Missing* (Dallas: Taylor Publishing Co., 1996).

7. Dan Rogers, letter to author, July 31, 1997.

8. F. C. Odds, *Candida and Candidiasis* (London: Baulien Tindall, 1990).

9. Stephen Edelson, "The Candida Albicans Mystery," *Health/Science Newsletter*, January 1997, p. 2.

10. Rob Stein, "Serotonin Differs between Sexes, Study Finds," *Washington Post*, May 18, 1997, p. 65.

11. Joan Mathews Larson and Keith W. Sehnert, *Seven Weeks to Sobriety* (New York: Ballantine Books, 1992), Introduction.

12. Ibid, p. 31.

Chapter 4

1. J. Trefil, "How the Body Defends Itself from the Risky Business of Living," *Smithsonian*, February 1997, pp. 43–49.

2. N. Zanichow and M. Saylor, "Oxygen Bars: A Breath of Fresh Air for Los Angeles," *Los Angeles Times*, May 31, 1997.

Chapter 5

1. Per Bjorntorp, "Stress and Weight Problems," *Healthy Weight Journal*, November/December 1996, pp. 20-21.

2. Richard L. Atkinson, "ASBP Has Major Presence and Participation, Dr. C. Everett Koop's First Obesity Treatment Guidance," *American Journal of Bariatric Physicians*, Fall 1996, pp. 11–14.

3. *Mayo Clinic Proceedings*, vol. 72, June 1997, p. 555.

4. Quoted in M. D. Lemonick, "The Mood Molecule," *Time*, September 15, 1997, pp. 74–82.

5. Richard L. Atkinson, "ASBP Has Major Presence and Participation, Dr. C. Everett Koop's First Obesity Treatment Guidance," *American Journal of Bariatric Physicians*, Fall 1996, pp. 11–14.

6. C. Everett Koop, *American Journal of Bariatric Physicians*, Fall 1996, pp. 11–14.

Chapter 6

1. Scott Walker, *Glimpses of God: Stories That Point the Way* (Minneapolis: Augsburg Books, 1997).

2. Ibid, p. 26.

3. Tamora Mahnerd and Keith W. Sehnert, *Keys to a New Life: Psychological and Biochemical Insights about Weight Loss* (Minneapolis: Renewal Resources, 1997).

4. N. Shute, "A Study for the Ages," *U.S. News and World Report*, June 9, 1997, pp. 67–80.

156   *Chapter 9*

1. Henry Cloud and John Townsend, *Boundaries: When to Say Yes and When to Say No to Take Control of Your Life* (Grand Rapids, Mich.: Zondervan Publishing House, 1992).
2. Ibid, p. 52.
3. Christine Winderlin and Keith W. Sehnert, *Candida-Related Complex: What Your Doctor Might Be Missing* (Dallas: Taylor Publishing Co., 1996).
4. William Crook, *The Yeast Connection and the Woman* (Jackson, Tenn.: Professional Books, 1995).

Chapter 12

1. Peter Jaret, "The National Sleep Debt," *USA Today*, January 3–5, 1991, pp. 4–5.
2. Ibid, p. 6.
3. K. Dowling, "Drivers on Legal Medication Pose Little Understood Risk," *Star Tribune* (Minneapolis), July 4, 1997, p. A-9.
4. Clarence Meyer, *The Herbalist* (Private publisher, Clarence Meyer, 1950).

Chapter 13

1. Kilmer S. McCully, *The Homocysteine Revolution* (New Canaan, Conn.: Keats Publishing, 1997).
2. Jeffrey Bland, *The 20-Day Rejuvenation Diet Program* (New Canaan, Conn.: Keats Publishing, 1997).
3. Ibid.
4. C. D. Davis and J. L. Greger, "Longitudinal Changes in Manganese Dependent Superoxide Dismutise and Other Indexes of Manganese and Iron Status in Women," *American Journal of Clinical Nutrition* 55 (1992): 747–52.
5. Jeffrey Bland, *The 20-Day Rejuvenation Diet Program* (New Canaan, Conn.: Keats Publishing, 1997), p. 201.

Chapter 14

1. Tamora Mahnerd and Keith W. Sehnert, *Keys to a New Life — Psychological and Biochemical Insights about Weight Loss* (Minneapolis: Renewal Resources, 1997).
2. Bonnie Liebman, "The Fight against Flab," *Nutrition Action Health Letter* 24, No. 10 (December 1997): 6–11.
3. Editorial: "Moving to Prevent Childhood Obesity," *American Journal of Bariatric Physicians*, Fall 1997: 22–23.

Chapter 15

1. L. Gale, "Not Just for Kids," *Star Tribune* (Minneapolis), December

27, 1997, pp. 1–2.

2. Phaedra Hise, "The Best Companies to Work For and What You Can Learn from Them," *Walking, the Magazine of Smart Health and Fitness,* September/October 1997, pp. 55–60.

3. Keith Sehnert, *Stress/Unstress* (Augsburg Publishing House, Minneapolis, 1981) p. 173.

4. Ibid, p. 174.

5. Ibid, p. 175.

6. Ibid, p. 175.

Chapter 16

1. Ron Fronk, personal correspondence, November 1997.

2. Victor Youcha, personal communication, November 1997.

3. Hans Selye, *The Stress of Life* (New York: McGraw-Hill, 1978) p. 60.

4. J. H. Wedge, *The Natural History of Spinal Degeneration: Managing Low Back Pain* (New York: Churchill Livingstone, 1983).

Chapter 17

1. Keith Sehnert, *Stress/Unstress* (Augsburg Publishing House, Minneapolis, 1981) p. 109.

2. Norman Sussman, "Neurochemistry of Serotonin and Depression," *Primary Psychiatry,* March 1995, pp. 28–35.

3. J. Wurtman, "Depression and Weight Gain: the Serotonin Connection," *Journal of Affective Disorders* 29 (1993): 183–92; L. N. Yatham and M. Steiner, "Neuroendocrine Probes of Serotonin and Serotoninergic Function: A Critical Review," *Life Science* 53 (1993): 447–63.

Chapter 18

1. Quoted in Claudia Wallis, "Faith and Healing," *Time,* June 24, 1996, p. 58.

2. Ibid, p. 61.

Chapter 19

1. "This Is My Father's World," text by M. D. Babcock, melody by F. L. Sheppard, *Lutheran Book of Worship* (Minneapolis: Augsburg Publishing House, 1978), #554.

Chapter 20

1. Tim O'Brien, "Stress Has a Way of Sneaking Up on Many of Us," *St. Paul Pioneer Press,* October 29, 1997, p. 5F.

2. Roland Seboldt, daily devotion in "Christ in Our Home," Minneapolis: Augsburg Publishing, June 29, 1995, p. 92.

RESOURCES

Suggested Reading

Brown, H. Jackson, Jr. *Life's Little Instruction Book*. Nashville, TN: Rutledge Hill Press, 1995.

Carlson, Richard. *Don't Sweat the Small Stuff: Simple Ways to Keep the Little Things from Taking Over Your Life*. New York: Hyperion, 1997.

Dossey, Larry. *Healing Words*. San Francisco: HarperSanFrancisco, 1996.

Maslach, Christina. *The Truth about Burnout*. San Francisco: Jossey-Bass, 1997.

Tubesing, Donald A., and Nancy Loving Tubesing. *Kicking Your Stress Habits: A Do-It Yourself Guide for Coping with Stress*. Duluth, MN: Whole Person Associates, 1981 (rev. 1989).

Seminars

Turning Point Resources
13027 N. 23rd Street
Phoenix, AZ 85022
(602) 404-2636

Stress Busters Seminars
4210 Fremont Ave. S.
Minneapolis, MN 55409
(612) 824-5134

Career Track, Training That Makes a Difference
MS2–3085 Center Green Drive
Boulder, CO 80301-5408
(800) 788-5478

Massage/Acupressure

The G-Jo Institute
P.O. Box 848060, Dept. T
Hollywood, FL 33084
(954) 791-1562

An excellent "how-to" book, *101 Essential Tips: Massage* by Nitya Lacroix (D.K. Publishing Inc., 95 Madison Ave., New York, NY 10016) is well worth reading.

Environmental Medicine

American Academy of Environmental Medicine
10 E. Randolph St.
New Hope, PA 18939
(215) 862-4544

Northern Plains Sustainable Agricultural Society
9824 79th Street S.E.
Fullerton, ND 58441-9725
(701) 883-5205
(organic farming)

Obesity/Weight Management

Tanita Master Distributor
Stellar Innovations, Inc.
James A. Hirtle
(800) 654-6611, fax: (310) 544-1001

Nutritional Supplements/Products

Swanson Health Products
P.O. Box 2803
Fargo, ND 58108
(800) 437-4148
(For glucosamine sulfate, CardioHelper, gingko biloba, St. John's Wort, and other products)

160 Quest IV Health Products, Inc.
2106 W. Pioneer Parkway, #131
Arlington, TX 76013
(817) 548-1296
(For Restores, use code #471282931)

U.A.S. Laboratories
5610 Rowland Road, #110
Minnetonka, MN 55434
(800) 422-3371
(For lactobacillus acidophilus products)

Videos

Master Motion Self-Study Course
Turning Point Resources
13027 N. 23rd Street
Phoenix, AZ 85022
(602) 404-2636